TestSmart

English • Math • Social Studies • Science

Grade 1

Printed in China

Contents

English

grade 1

Contents

Math

Contents

Social Studies

Science

TestSmart

English

Test 1

- reading comprehension

Read the letter.

Grandma's Farm

Dear Mom and Dad,

I am having so much fun on Grandma's farm. Each day we feed the pigs, cows, and chickens. Today, Grandma and I are going to pick apples. We will use the apples to bake a pie. I can't wait to eat it!

See you next Tuesday.

Love,
Pam

A. Check the animals on Grandma's farm. Put a cross for the ones that are not. (2 marks each)

10

Date:

B. Check the correct answers. (2 marks each)

/10

1. _____ writes this letter.

(A) 

(B) 

(C) 

2. This is a letter for _____ .

(A) Pam (B) Grandma (C) Dad and Mom

3. Pam is going to pick _____ today.

(A) pears (B) apples (C) strawberries

4. Pam will be home next _____ .

(A) Monday (B) Tuesday (C) Thursday

5. Grandma will bake a _____ .

(A) pie (B) cake (C) pizza

Total

/20

Test 2

English

- **beginning consonants**
- **ending consonants**

A. Check the correct answers. (1 mark each)

2

1. ____ are consonants.

   A. **A**, **e**, **i**, **o**, and **u**

   B. **C**, **g**, **m**, **s**, and **t**

   C. **Oo**, **ou**, **aw**, and **ow**

2. The ____ consonant of "stick" is "k".

   A. beginning

   B. middle

   C. ending

B. Look at each picture. Circle the correct consonant for the word. (1 mark each)

6

1. 

   fo | s | x |

2. 

   | c | g | ap

3. 

   | l | n | ine

4. 

   cu | b | p |

5. 

   | f | v | an

6. 

   | s | z | eal

C. Look at each picture and read the word. One consonant is wrong. Correct and rewrite each word. (2 marks each)

12

1.

______

2.

______

3.

______

4.

______

5.

______

6.

______

Total 20

BONUS

Each word below begins and ends with the same consonant. Fill in the missing letters.

1. ____ ic ____

2. ____ oa ____

3. ____ in ____

Bonus /2

Test 3

- reading comprehension

English

Read the story.

Where Is Marvin?

It is time for Fiona to feed her pets. First, she feeds Henry and Rosa the Hamsters. Then Buster the Goldfish gets his lunch. After that is Gregory the Snake's turn. Next in line is Marvin the Caterpillar. But...where is Marvin? Marvin is missing! Fiona looks under the table and in the cupboard. She checks Gregory's cage. Where could Marvin be? Marvin? Marvin? Marvin! There you are! You're flying, Marvin!

A. Write the names of Fiona's pets. (1 mark each)

5

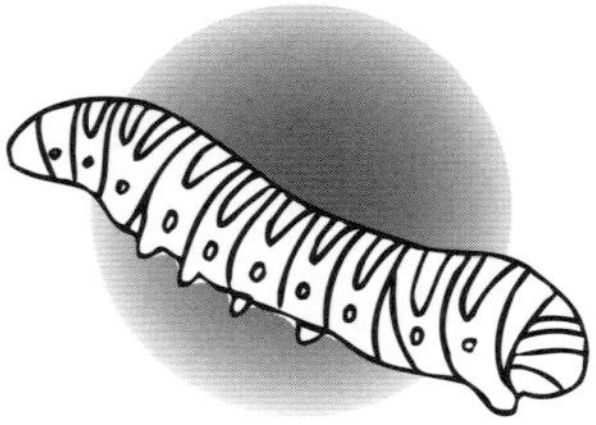

1. ____________

2. ____________

3. ____________

4. ____________

5. ____________

B. Write "T" for the true sentences and "F" for the false ones. (2 marks each)

12

1. Fiona has five pets. ______
2. It is dinner time. ______
3. Marvin the Caterpillar is missing. ______
4. Fiona keeps her snake in a cage. ______
5. Fiona finally finds Marvin in the cupboard. ______
6. Marvin can now fly. ______

C. Circle what Marvin is now. (3 marks)

3

Marvin

A

B

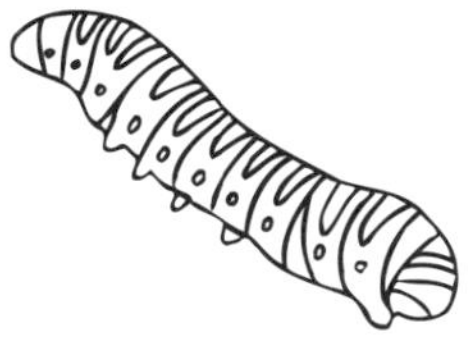

C

D

Total

20

Test 4

- short vowels
- long vowels

English

A. Check the correct answers. (1 mark each)

2

1. ____ are vowels.

   (A) **A**, **e**, **i**, **o**, and **u**

   (B) **B**, **d**, **h**, **m**, and **v**

   (C) **Sl**, **br**, **th**, and **ch**

2. A long vowel sounds the same as you say the ____ .

   (A) consonant

   (B) letter

   (C) word

B. Look at each picture. Fill in the missing vowel.

(1 mark each)

4

1. 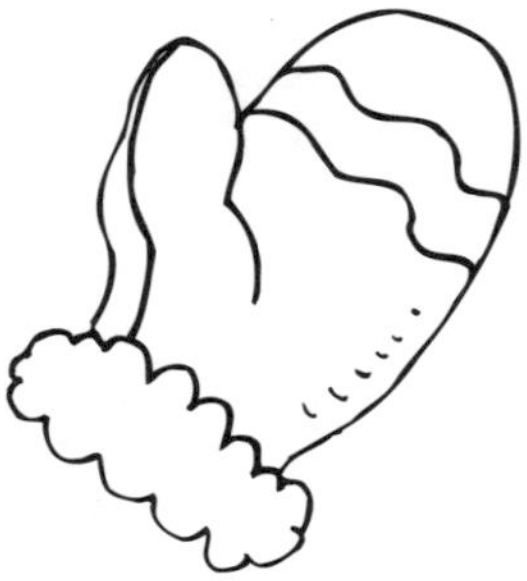 m ___ tten

2.  b ___ sket

3.  cl ___ ck

4. 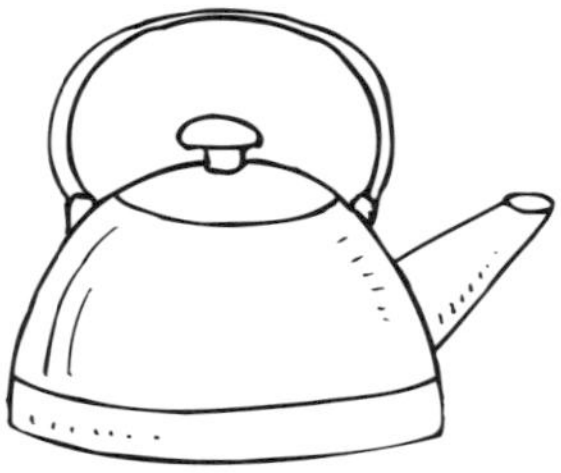 k ___ ttle

C. Read the words in each group. Circle the word with a long vowel sound. (2 marks each)

14

1.
can hare
cane
sand track

2.
prize drink
prince
pin swim

3.
cone
love
pond
bottle
pot

4.
cup duck cub cube umbrella

5.
tent bench
sweat
sweep desert

6.
clever mug
cute
elf uncle

7.
actor
acorn
add
apple
alarm

Total
20

BONUS

Some words with the long "u" sound do not contain the letter "u". Circle the words with the long "u" sound below.

blew moose boat
good jewel view

Bonus
/ 2

Test 5

- reading comprehension

Read the story.

The Buried Treasure

I had a dream last night. My sister Katherine and I were pirates looking for buried treasure. We set out in a big boat to find the treasure. We sailed across an ocean to where the palm trees grew. We saw many amazing things, like a parrot that talked like Katherine and flowers that were as big as dining tables! We had a lot of fun, but we did not find any treasure.

A. Check the things that appeared in the dream. Put a cross for the ones that did not. (1 mark each)

6

Date:

B. Fill in the blanks to complete the sentences.
(2 marks each)

14

flowers ocean parrot pirates
dream treasure buried

1. Last night, I had a ______________ .

2. My sister and I were ______________ .

3. We sailed across an ______________ .

4. We were looking for ______________ treasure.

5. There was a ______________ that talked like my sister.

6. We saw ______________ as big as dining tables.

7. We did not find any ______________ in the end.

Total

20

Test 6

English

- **rhyming words**

A. Check the correct answers. (1 mark each)

2

1. Rhyming words are words that ______ the same sound.

   (A) have
   (B) begin with
   (C) end with

2. ______ are rhyming pairs.

   (A) "Best" and "vest"
   (B) "Pin" and "pan"
   (C) "Fog" and "fork"

B. Read the words in each group. Cross out the word that does not rhyme with the others.
(2 marks each)

10

1. fall floor hall ball doll
2. mail tale rail snail fill
3. near here pier rare deer
4. send tent tend bend mend
5. band hand wand sand land

Date:

C. Look at the thing in each picture. Write a word that rhymes with that thing. (2 marks each)

8

Rhyming Pairs

1.

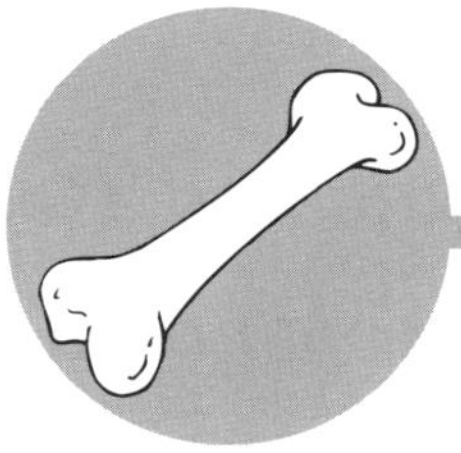

2.

3.

4.

Total

20

BONUS

Write four words that rhyme with "sing".

Bonus

/2

Test 7

- reading comprehension

English

Read the story.

Winter Fun

Hi, my name is Darren. Last Saturday, Dad and I made two snowmen in the front yard. Dad called his snowman King Kong. I named my snowman Ping Pong.

King Kong was huge and Ping Pong was cute. Dad put two chocolate cookies on King Kong for the eyes and a big potato for the nose. I had two big, black buttons for Ping Pong's eyes and a long carrot for his nose. Ping Pong's nose was as long as Pinocchio's!

A. Label the snowmen. (1 mark each)

2

B. Write "T" for the true sentences and "F" for the false ones. (1 mark each)

6

1. Darren and his dad made snowmen last Saturday. ______
2. They made snowmen in the front yard. ______
3. Dad named the two snowmen. ______
4. Ping Pong was huge. ______
5. Ping Pong had a long nose. ______
6. They made a third snowman and named it Pinocchio. ______

C. Write what Darren and his dad used to make the snowmen. (3 marks each)

12

Darren's Snowman

- snow
- *1.* ______
- *2.* ______

Dad's Snowman

- snow
- *3.* ______
- *4.* ______

Total

20

Test 8

English

- **nouns**
- **common and proper nouns**

A. Check the correct answers. (1 mark each)

2

1. A common noun names ____ .

   (A) a specific person, place, or thing

   (B) any person, place, or thing

   (C) a common thing

2. "Anna" and "Toronto" are examples of ____ .

   (A) common nouns

   (B) simple nouns

   (C) proper nouns

B. Circle the nouns in each sentence. (2 marks each)

8

1. The cat runs after the mouse.
2. There are many flowers in the garden.
3. The girl is drawing a picture.
4. This story is about a king.

C. Write the proper nouns in the correct places.
(1 mark each)

4

	Common Noun	Proper Noun
David	city	1. ______
Barbie	boy	2. ______
Ottawa	movie	3. ______
WALL-E	doll	4. ______

D. Look at the pictures. Put the letters in order and write the common nouns. (2 marks each)

6

1. 

pheeltan

______

2. 

brliray

______

3. 

ctdoro

______

Total

20

Test 9

- **reading comprehension**

A. Fill in the blanks in the poem with the given words. (1 mark each)

5

dogs	**bee**	**crow**
frogs	**bear**	

What Is It?

There are footprints in a row.

Who made them? Do you know?

Oh! It's just a 1. ____________ .

Something's buzzing in the tree.

It's moving fast. Can you see?

Dear me! It's a 2. ____________ !

Something's growling in its lair.

Is it big? Should we beware?

Over there! It's a 3. ____________ !

Date:

What just hopped onto the logs?

I can't tell.

Are they 4. ________________ ?

Look closer.

It's a couple of 5. ________________ .

B. Answer the questions. (5 marks each)

15

1. What did the bird make?

____

2. What is buzzing in the tree?

____

3. How many frogs are there?

____

____

Total

20

Test 10

- **singular nouns**
- **plural nouns**

A. Check the correct answers. (1 mark each)

/ 2

1. A ______ noun names one person or thing.

   (A) singular
   (B) plural
   (C) collective

2. We form some plural nouns by adding ______ to the singular nouns.

   (A) "s" or "d"
   (B) "s" or "es"
   (C) "es" or "ed"

B. Circle the words that match the pictures. (2 marks each)

/ 6

1.

duck

ducks

2.

house

houses

3.

tomato

tomatoes

Date:

C. Fill in the blanks with the given nouns. Change the nouns to plural when needed. (2 marks each)

12

squirrel boot park sister sandwich story

1. Sharon and Maggie are my ____________ .
2. I have a new pair of ____________ .
3. There is a ____________ in the backyard.
4. My grandma makes tasty ____________ .
5. That ____________ is really interesting.
6. There are a few ____________ in the city.

Total

20

BONUS

Write the plural form of each noun below.

1. fairy ____________
2. leaf ____________
3. salmon ____________

Bonus

/ 2

Test 11

- reading comprehension

Read the story.

All about Me

My name is Jill, and I live at 10 Maple Street. I live with my parents and my brother, Chris. My birthday is May 15 and my brother's birthday is June 24. I go to Parkside School. My teacher's name is Miss Green.

I went to visit my grandpa and grandma in New York last summer. I had a good time, but I was happy to get back to Canada.

I have a best friend named Angela. We love to ride our bikes and play at the park. I hope you enjoyed reading all about me.

A. Check the things that Jill and her friend like doing. (1 mark each)

2

A

B

C

B. Fill in the blanks to complete the chart about Jill.
(2 marks each)

14

All about Jill

Address: 10 ____________________ Street

Birthday: ____________________

Brother's Name: ____________________

Brother's Birthday: ____________________

School: ____________________ School

Teacher's Name: ____________________

Best Friend's Name: ____________________

C. Give short answers to the questions. (2 marks each)

4

1. When did Jill visit her grandparents?

____

2. Where do Jill's grandparents live?

____

Total

20

Test 12

- **articles**

A. Check the correct answers. (1 mark each) 2

1. An article is used ____ .

   (A) before a noun
   (B) after a noun
   (C) with a pronoun

2. The article ____ can be used with both singular and plural nouns.

   (A) "a"
   (B) "an"
   (C) "the"

B. Write "a" or "an" for each group of pictures. (2 marks each) 4

1.

2.

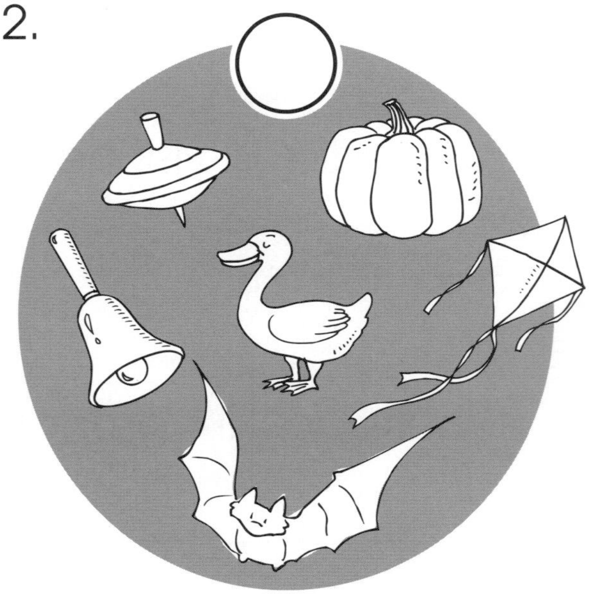

C. Circle the correct articles to complete the sentences. (2 marks each)

14

1. I eat a / an orange every day.
2. Never look directly at a / the sun.
3. There is a / an eagle flying outside.
4. How tall is a / the CN Tower?
5. Do you know an / the author of this book?
6. We need to buy a / the cake for Dad's birthday.
7. A / An bear can climb trees.

Total 20

BONUS

Write "a" or "an" for the nouns.

1. ______ unicorn
2. ______ hour

Bonus /2

Test 13

- writing

A. Look at each picture. Put the words in order to form a sentence about the picture.

(3 marks each)

12

1. 

likes / drinking / kitten / milk / The / .

____

____

2. 

is / The / brightly / sun / shining / .

____

____

3. 

games / play / recess / We / at / ball / .

____

____

4. 

Kate / to / This / book / belongs / .

____

____

Date:

B. Write a sentence about each picture with the given words. (4 marks each)

8

* Ask your mom, dad, or teacher to mark this part. You can also mark it yourself.

1.

Sam James

making mask

2.

Tim walking

dog rain

Total

20

Test 14

- reading comprehension

English

Read the recipe.

Delicious
Fruity Smoothie

Ingredients:

- 2 bananas
- 6 ice cubes
- 1 cup fruit yogurt
- 1 cup orange juice

Steps:

1. Peel the bananas and carefully cut them into chunks on a cutting board. (Ask your mom or dad to help you.)
2. Put the banana chunks and the ice cubes into the blender.
3. Pour the yogurt into the blender.
4. Pour the orange juice into the blender.
5. Blend until it is smooth.
6. Pour the smoothie into two glasses and enjoy!

Date:

A. Check the ingredients for the smoothie. Put a cross for the ones that are not. (1 mark each)

8

B. Fill in the blanks with words from the recipe.
(2 marks each)

12

1. You need ____________ yogurt to make the smoothie.

2. Cut the bananas on a cutting ____________ .

3. Ask your parents to help you cut the ____________ .

4. Pour the yogurt and juice into the ____________ .

5. Blend everything until it is ____________ .

6. This recipe makes ____________ glasses of smoothie.

Total
20

English

Test 15

- **subject pronouns**

A. Check the correct answers. (1 mark each)

2

1. A subject pronoun replaces ______ in a sentence.

   (A) a verb

   (B) a subject

   (C) an object

2. ______ are examples of subject pronouns.

   (A) "I" and "she"

   (B) "Me" and "her"

   (C) "Mine" and "hers"

B. Match the subject pronouns with the words.

(1 mark each)

4

1. he •
2. she •
3. it •
4. they •

- Karen
- the dogs over there
- the waiter
- this book

C. Write "I", "you", "we", or "they" for each picture.
(1 mark each)

4

D. Fill in the blanks with the correct subject pronouns.
(2 marks each)

10

1. Mom baked a big pie. ______________ was yummy.
2. Let's go to the beach. ______________ can play volleyball there.
3. I can't tell you the answer. ______________ have to solve the question yourself.
4. I like my sister. ______________ is also my best friend.
5. Please feed the dogs. ______________ look hungry.

Total

20

Test 16

- reading comprehension

Read the story.

Chickadee

The sun is shining. Chickadee looks out from his nest. He sees green leaves on long branches. He sees a red butterfly. He sees a buzzing bee.

Chickadee looks down at the ground. The forest floor is a long way down. But Chickadee is not scared. He flutters his wings like the leaves. He flutters his wings like the butterfly. He flutters his wings like the bee.

Chickadee lands on a branch. "Chick-a-dee-dee-dee-dee-dee-dee-dee," he sings happily to the butterfly and the bee.

A. Which one below is Chickadee? Circle the correct picture. (2 marks)

2

Date:

B. Draw lines to match the words with the pictures. (2 marks each)

10

1. long •
2. red •
3. green •
4. shining •
5. buzzing •

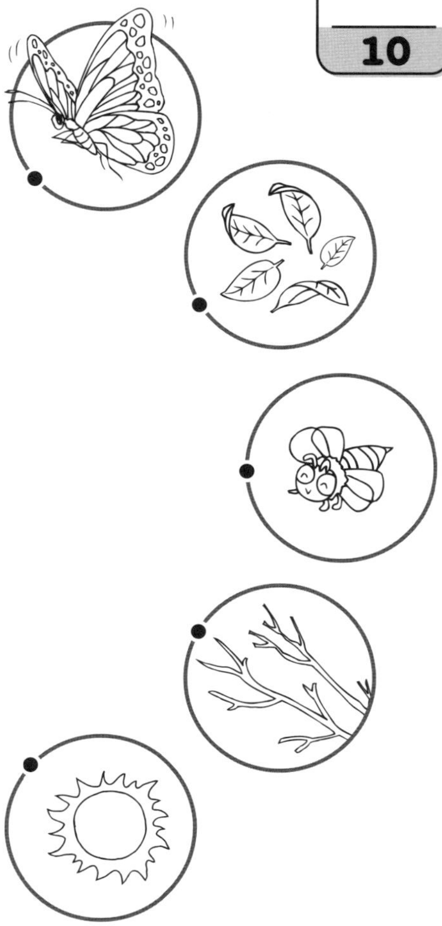

C. Answer the questions. (4 marks each)

8

1. Where does Chickadee live?

____

2. Which sentence tells you that Chickadee lives high up?

____

____

Total

20

Test 17

- **verbs**

A. Check the correct answers. (1 mark each)

2

1. Most verbs are ____ words.

   (A) location
   (B) connecting
   (C) action

2. ____ are verbs.

   (A) "Song" and "egg"
   (B) "Eat" and "ask"
   (C) "Cute" and "fast"

B. Circle the verbs in the sentences. (1 mark each)

6

1. My mom drives me to school every day.
2. Colour your picture with crayons.
3. Please buy a carton of milk on your way home.
4. We can borrow books from the library.
5. Crunchy, my pet dog, sleeps in my room.
6. Bees collect nectar from flowers.

Date:

C. Write the correct verbs for the actions in the picture. (2 marks each)

12

slide   jump   swing   clap   push   run

1 ______________

2 ______________

3 ______________

4 ______________

5 ______________

6 ______________

Total

20

BONUS

Rewrite the sentence replacing the underlined verb with another verb of the same meaning.

All classes <u>gather</u> in the hall before the outing.

____

____

Bonus

/ 2

Test 18

- reading comprehension

Read the story.

The King and Queen's Quilts

Once upon a time, there was a queen. She lived in a castle with the king. They lived a quiet life and were very happy. One day they had a quarrel. They went to the village to buy a new quilt. The queen wanted a red one, but the king wanted a blue one.

The quarrel went on for quite a while. Finally, the king had the answer to the question. They got two quilts – one red and one blue. They quit fighting and lived happily ever after.

A. Check the word for each picture. (1 mark each)

3

1. 

Ⓐ king

Ⓑ queen

Ⓒ quilt

2. 

Ⓐ king

Ⓑ queen

Ⓒ quarrel

3. 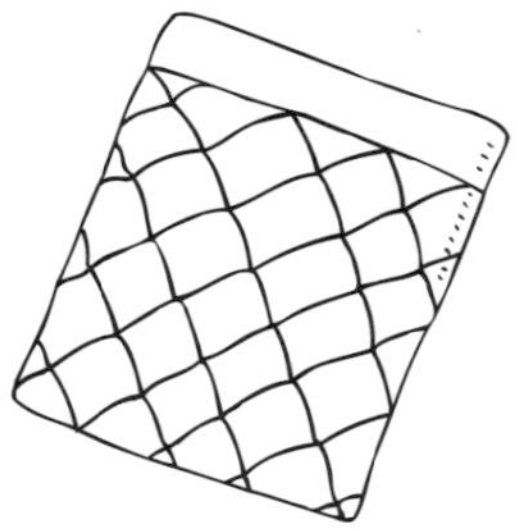

Ⓐ quarrel

Ⓑ castle

Ⓒ quilt

B. Circle the correct words to complete the sentences. (2 marks each)

12

1. The king and the queen lived in a castle / village .

2. The king and the queen lived a new / happy life.

3. They went to the castle / village to buy a new quilt.

4. The king wanted a red / blue quilt.

5. The queen wanted a red / blue quilt.

6. In the end, the king / queen had the answer to the question.

C. Answer the question. (5 marks)

5

How was the problem solved in the end?

Total

20

Test 19

- **adjectives**

A. Check the correct answers. (1 mark each)

2

1. An adjective is a word that describes ______ .

   (A) a person, place, or thing
   (B) an action
   (C) "how often"

2. Words for ______ are not adjectives.

   (A) colour and number
   (B) size and shape
   (C) time and location

B. Cross out the word that is not an adjective in each group. (2 marks each)

6

1. **green** **blue** **colour** **pink** **yellow**

2. **round** **disk** **five** **oval** **three**

3. **small** **tall** **huge** **tiny** **height**

Date:

C. Write the correct adjectives to describe the animals.
(6 marks each)

12

1.

black
cute
short
tiny

- a __________ dog
- a __________ nose
- __________ legs

2.

long
big
sharp
red

- a __________ elephant
- a __________ tail
- __________ tusks

Total

20

BONUS

Circle the adjectives with the same meaning.

huge wide enormous

deep giant

gigantic tiny large

Bonus

/ 2

Test 20

- **reading comprehension**

Read the story.

Sense Hike

Anna goes on a sense hike. With her eyes, she can see a beautiful rainbow. With her ears, she hears the sound of birds singing. With her hands, she touches the rough bark of the big oak tree.

When Anna gets home, she can smell the pizza in the oven with her nose. For dessert, she eats a bowl of chocolate ice cream with her mouth. It tastes great!

A. Draw the correct pictures in the boxes.
(1 mark each)

___ / 5

1. Anna sees with her ☐ .
2. Anna hears with her ☐ .
3. Anna touches with her ☐ .
4. Anna smells with her ☐ .
5. Anna tastes with her ☐ .

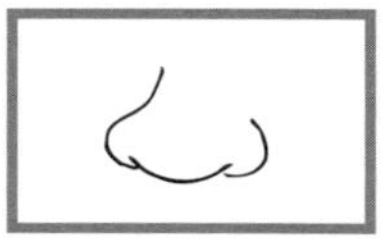

Date:

B. Fill in the blanks with words from the story.
(1 mark each)

___ / 7

1. Anna sees a ________________ .

2. Anna ________________ birds singing.

3. Anna ________________ the bark of a tree.

4. The bark of the tree is ________________ .

5. Anna smells a ________________ .

6. Anna eats ice cream for ________________ .

7. The ice cream ________________ great.

C. Answer the questions. (4 marks each)

___ / 8

1. What tree does Anna touch?

____

2. Where is the pizza?

____

Total

___ / 20

Test 21

English

- **prepositions**

A. Check the correct answers. (1 mark each)

2

1. A preposition tells the ______ of someone or something.

   (A) location

   (B) action

   (C) state

2. ______ are prepositions.

   (A) "A" and "the"

   (B) "Or" and "but"

   (C) "In" and "at"

B. Circle the correct preposition for each picture. (2 marks each)

6

1.

in / under

2.

on / behind

3.

behind / under

Date:

C. Fill in the blanks with the correct prepositions to complete the sentences. (2 marks each)

12

in
on
above
under
beside
behind

1. The butterfly is ______________ the flower.

2. The snail is ______________ the flower.

3. The bee is flying ______________ the basket.

4. There are two fairies ______________ the basket.

5. Some apples are ______________ the fairies.

6. There are some small flowers ______________ the basket.

Total

20

Some prepositions tell when someone does something. Fill in the blanks with the correct prepositions.

______________ five o'clock

______________ Halloween night

Bonus

/2

Test 22

- reading comprehension

Read the messages.

Who Is Messaging You?

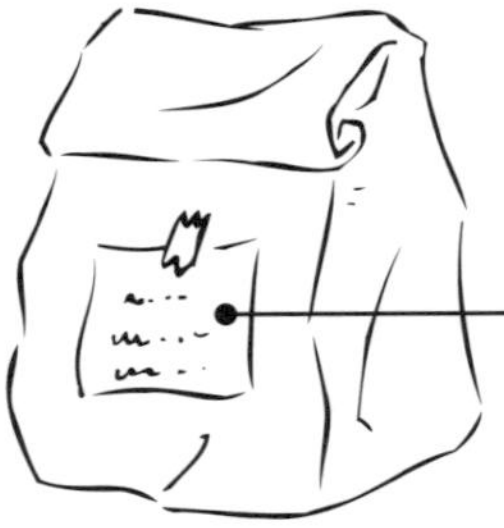

Sam,

I made your favourite sandwich.
Have a good day at school!
See you at home.

Love,
Dad

Jen,

Let's meet in front of the school.

See you soon! =)

\- Dan

Dear John,

I will be getting home late tonight. I need to pick up some snacks at the store.

Dinner is in the fridge.

Love,
Mom

A. Circle the incorrect word. Write the correct word on the line. (2 marks each)

8

1. Sam's dad ate Sam's favourite sandwich.

____

2. Dan wants to meet Jen in front of the park.

____

3. John's mom will be getting home early.

____

4. John's mom needs to pick up some drinks at the store.

____

B. Answer the questions. (4 marks each)

12

1. Who messaged Jen?

____

2. Who made Sam's favourite sandwich?

____

3. Where is John's dinner?

____

Total

20

Test 23

English

- **types of sentences**

A. Check the correct answers. (1 mark each)

2

1. A/An ______ sentence asks a question about someone or something.

   A telling
   B asking
   C surprising

2. A/An ______ sentence shows strong feelings.

   A telling
   B asking
   C surprising

B. Read each group of words. If they form a sentence, check ☺. If not, check ☹. (1 mark each)

4

Sentences

1. Let's go. ☺ — ☹
2. The apples in the basket. ☺ — ☹
3. This box is heavy. ☺ — ☹
4. His name. ☺ — ☹

C. Sort the sentences into the correct boxes. Write the letters. (2 marks each)

14

A Do you want to join us?

B There is a big fountain in the middle of the garden.

C Is there a boy named Karl in your class?

D Wow! That's a great idea!

E How wonderful!

F I visit Grandma and Grandpa every Sunday.

G Can we start now?

Telling Sentences

Asking Sentences

Surprising Sentences

Total

20

BONUS

The following sentences all begin with "What", but they are different types of sentences. Write the type of sentence for each of them.

T – telling sentence **A** – asking sentence **S** – surprising sentence

Bonus

/ 2

1. What a lovely day! ______
2. What you say is right. ______
3. What is a kangaroo? ______

Test 24

English

- reading comprehension

Read the story.

Pancake Breakfast

Rob sat at the table waiting for his favourite breakfast food – pancakes! His grandma came to visit and she is very good at making pancakes.

Grandma gave Rob a big pancake. Rob smeared butter and poured sweet maple syrup on it. He took a huge bite, and it was just delicious.

Grandma promised to teach Rob how to make pancakes. Soon, Rob will be able to make pancake breakfasts for his family.

A. Label the picture. (1 mark each)

3

A ____________________

B ____________________

C ____________________

Date:

B. Write the sentences in order. (2 marks each)

12

- Grandma made pancakes.
- Rob ate the pancake.
- Grandma gave Rob a pancake.
- Rob smeared butter on the pancake.
- Grandma came to visit.
- Rob poured maple syrup on the pancake.

1. ______
2. ______
3. ______
4. ______
5. ______
6. ______

C. Answer the question. (5 marks)

5

What did Grandma promise?

______

______

Total

20

Test 25

English

- **punctuation**
- **capitalization**

A. Check the correct answers. (1 mark each)

___ / 2

1. ____ sentences begin with a capital letter.

   A No
   B Some
   C All

2. An asking sentence ends with ____ .

   A a period
   B a question mark
   C an exclamation mark

B. Put the correct punctuation marks in the circles.

(1 mark each)

___ / 6

1. I keep my toys in a toy box ◯
2. Watch out ◯
3. How interesting this story is ◯
4. How can we get to the resort ◯
5. Are there any koala bears in Canada ◯
6. The clown has a big red nose ◯

C. Write what the pictures are. Use capital letters where needed. (1 mark each)

3

a ______________

a ______________

the ______________

cn tower
spider web
train station
christmas tree
building

D. Rewrite the sentences using the correct punctuation and capitalization. (3 marks each)

9

1. jasmine and i live on the same street

____

2. can i go to niagara falls with you, dad

____

3. what an exciting game

____

Total

20

Test 26

English

- **writing**

* Ask your mom, dad, or teacher to mark this test. You can also mark it yourself.

A. Look at the picture. Write five sentences about it. (10 marks)

10

1. ______________________________

____

2. ______________________________

____

3. ______________________________

____

4. ______________________________

____

5. ______________________________

____

Date:

B. Write a paragraph about yourself. (10 marks)

10

Here are some questions to help you:

- What is your name?
- When were you born?
- Where were you born?
- Where do you live?
- With whom do you live?
- Do you have any brothers or sisters?
- If yes, what are their names?
- What is the name of your school?
- What is your favourite food?
- What do you like doing?
- Who is your best friend?
- What do you like doing with your best friend?

Total

20

My Test Record

Test 1
- reading comprehension

/20

Test 2
- beginning consonants
- ending consonants

/20

Test 3
- reading comprehension

/20

Test 4
- short vowels
- long vowels

/20

Test 5
- reading comprehension

/20

Test 6
- rhyming words

/20

Test 7
- reading comprehension

/20

Test 8
- nouns
- common and proper nouns

/20

Test 9
- reading comprehension

/20

Test 10
- singular nouns
- plural nouns

/20

Test 11
- reading comprehension

/20

Test 12
- articles

/20

Test 13

- writing

___ / 20

Test 14

- reading comprehension

___ / 20

Test 15

- subject pronouns

___ / 20

Test 16

- reading comprehension

___ / 20

Test 17

- verbs

___ / 20

Test 18

- reading comprehension

___ / 20

Test 19

- adjectives

___ / 20

Test 20

- reading comprehension

___ / 20

Test 21

- prepositions

___ / 20

Test 22

- reading comprehension

___ / 20

Test 23

- types of sentences

___ / 20

Test 24

- reading comprehension

___ / 20

Test 25

- punctuation
- capitalization

___ / 20

Test 26

- writing

___ / 20

TestSmart

Math

Test 1

- numbers and number words

A. Count the number of objects. Write the numbers. (1 mark each)

10

1.

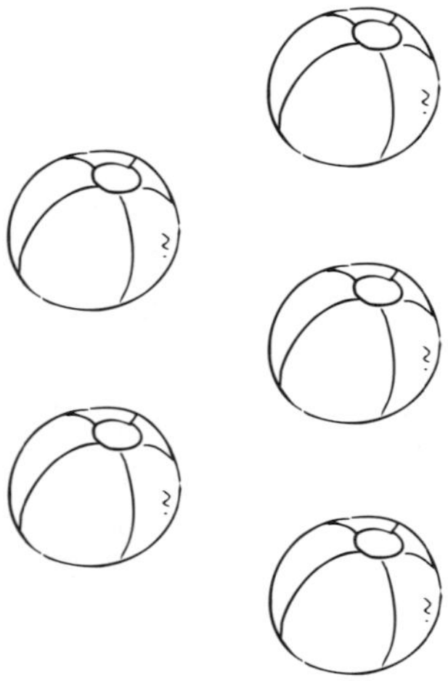

______

2.

______

3.

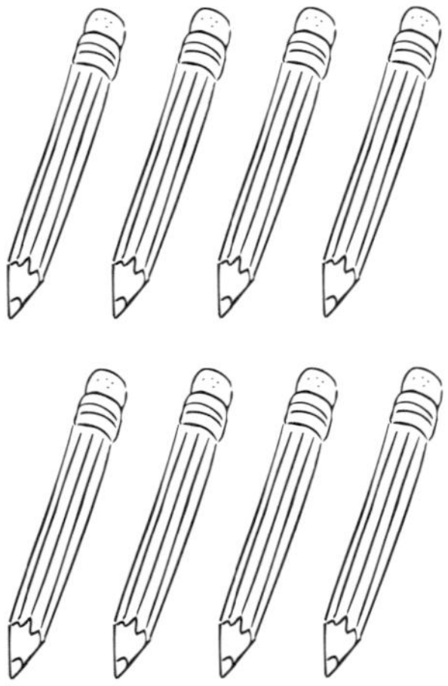

______

4.  ______

5.  ______

6.  ______

7.  ______

8.  ____________

9.  ____________

10.  ____________

B. Write the number words. (1 mark each)

____ / 10

1 ____________

2 ____________

3 ____________

4 ____________

5 ____________

6 ____________

7 ____________

8 ____________

9 ____________

10 ____________

Total ____ / 20

Test 2

- more or less

A. Draw arrays to show more or less. (2 marks each)

/4

1.

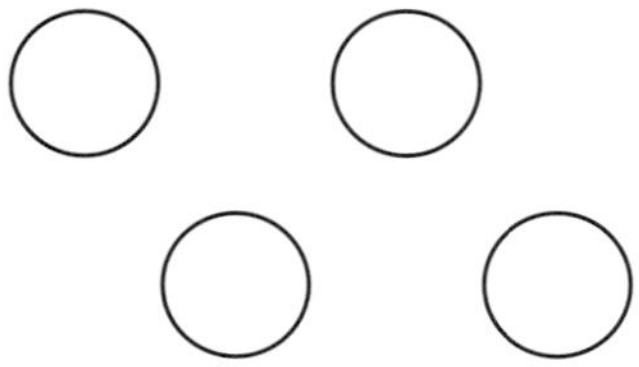

Show 2 more:

2.

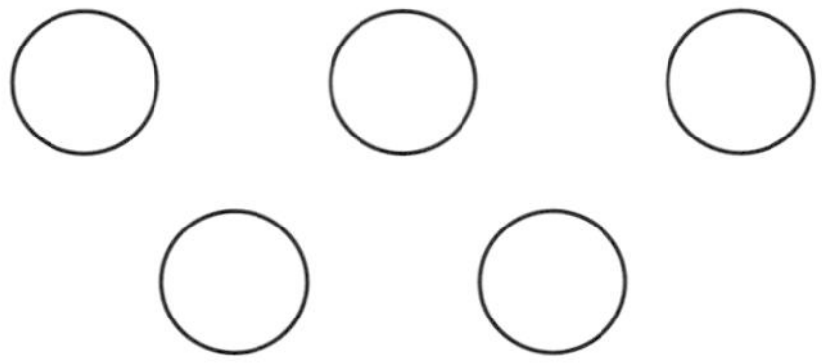

Show 1 less:

B. Check the correct sentences. (2 marks each)

/4

1.

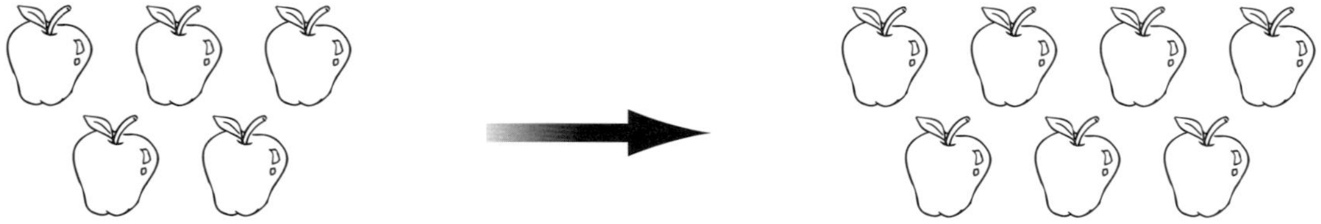

(A) Shows 2 more. (B) Shows 1 less.

2.

(A) Shows 2 less. (B) Shows 2 more.

Date:

C. Draw arrays and fill in the blanks. (2 marks each)

6

1. 2 more than 3 is ________ .

→

2. 1 less than 4 is ________ .

→

3. 2 less than 6 is ________ .

→

D. Find the answers. (3 marks each)

6

1. 1 more than 3

____

2. 2 less than 7

____

Total 20

BONUS

Is "3 more than 4" the same as "4 more than 3"?

____

Bonus / 2

Test 3

• more than 5

A. Check the groups that have more than 5 objects. (1 mark each)

2

(A)

(B)

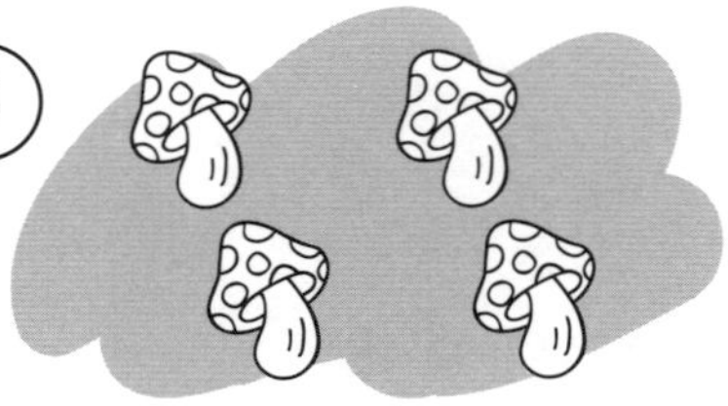

(C)

(D)

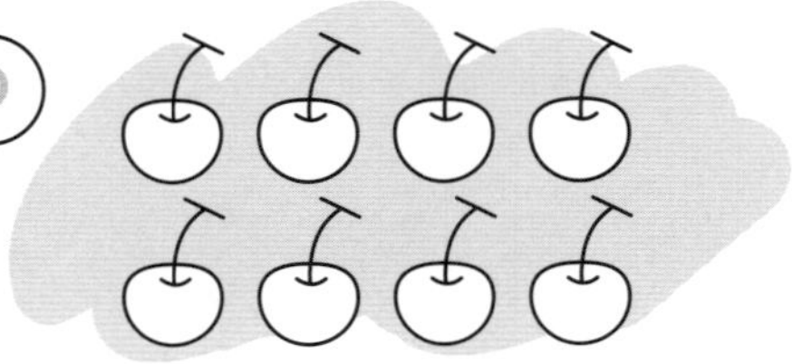

B. Circle 5 objects and fill in the blanks.
(2 marks each)

6

1\.

6 is ____ more than 5.

2\.

8 is ____ more than 5.

3\.

7 is ____ more than 5.

C. Draw arrays to help you fill in the blanks. (3 marks each)

12

1.

_____ is 3 more than 5.

2.

_____ is 2 more than 5.

3.

_____ is 5 more than 5.

4.

_____ is 1 more than 5.

BONUS

Check the number that is 10 more than 5.

(A) 5
(B) 10
(C) 15

Total
20

Bonus
/ 2

Test 4

- less than 10

A. Check the sentence that describes the counters. (2 marks each)

6

1. 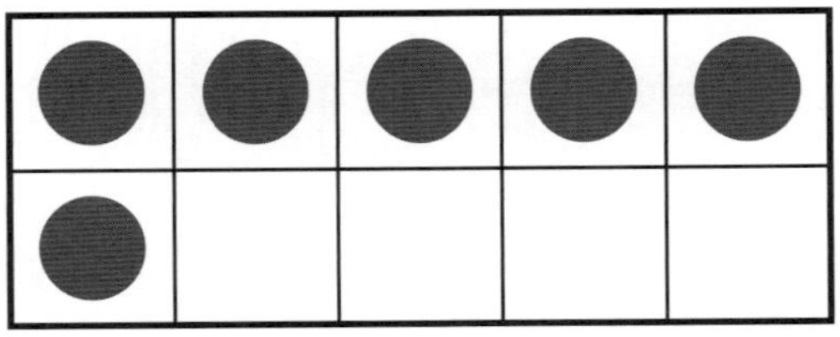

Ⓐ 6 is 4 less than 10.
Ⓑ 6 is 2 less than 10.

2. 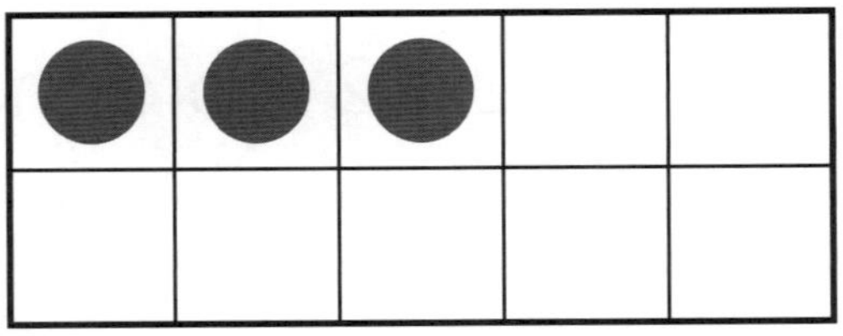

Ⓐ 7 is 10 less than 3.
Ⓑ 3 is 7 less than 10.

3. 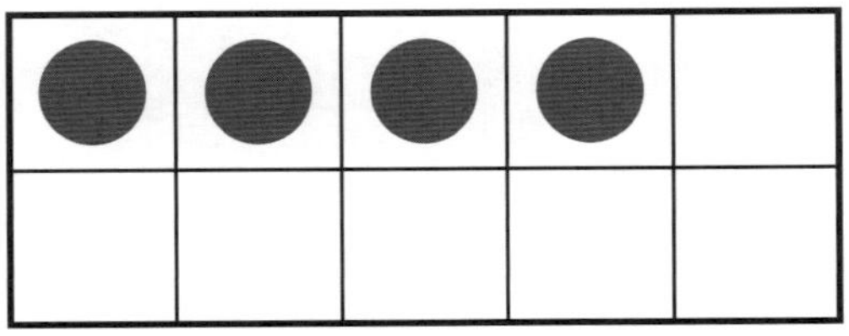

Ⓐ 4 is 6 less than 10.
Ⓑ 10 is 4 less than 6.

B. Draw counters and fill in the blanks.
(2 marks each)

4

1. 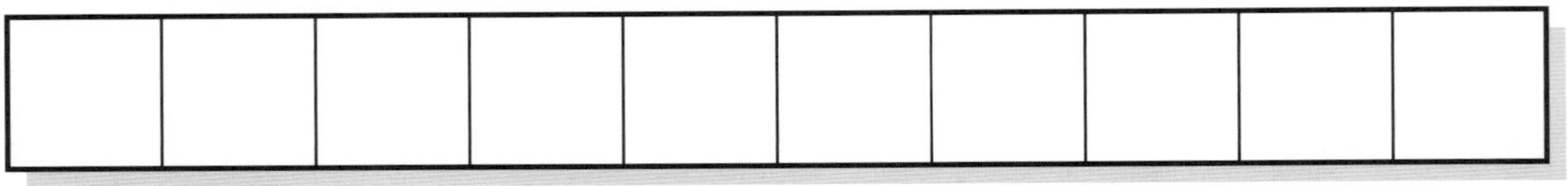

3 is ______ less than 10.

2. 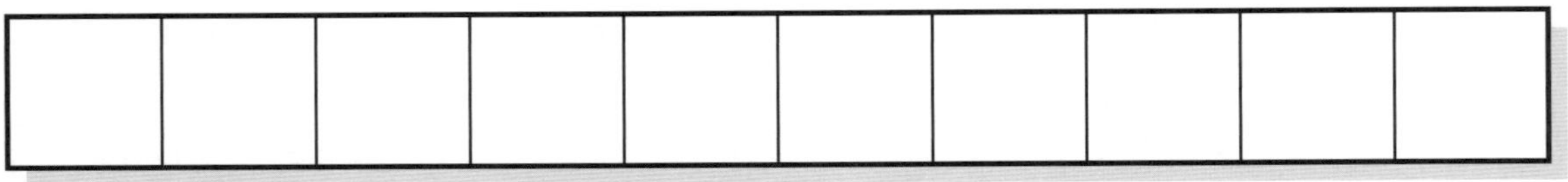

______ is 2 less than 10.

C. Write a sentence to describe each group of objects. (2 marks each)

10

1.

_____ is _____ less than 10.

2.

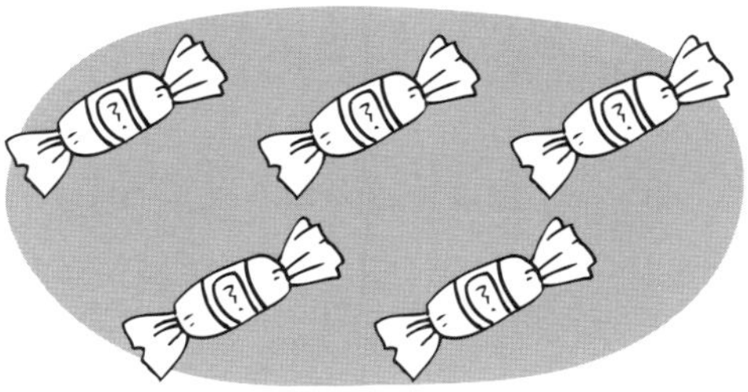

____

3.

____

4.

____

5.

____

Total

20

Math

Test 5

- addition

A. Find the total number of fruits. (1 mark each)

/3

1.

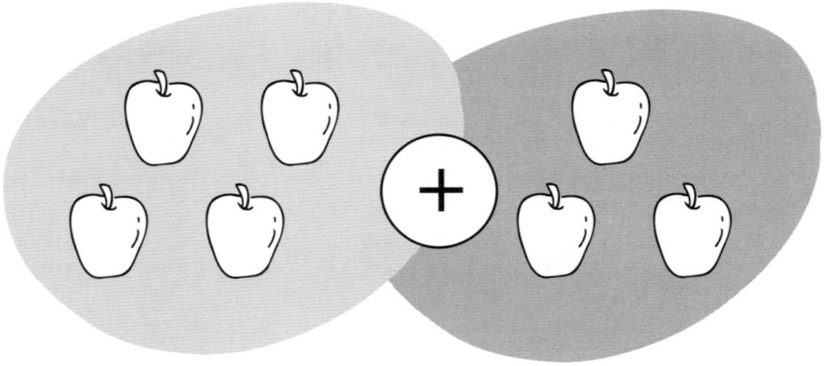

= ______ 

2.

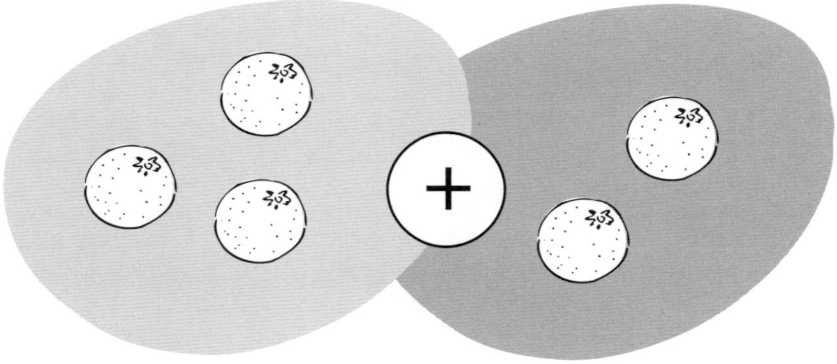

= ______ 

3.

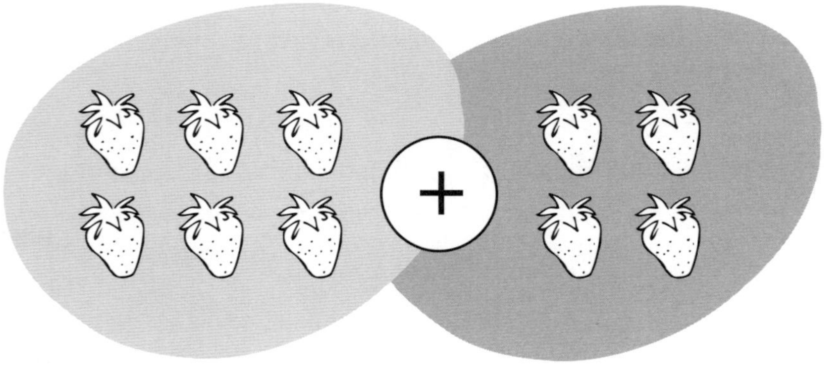

= ______ 

Date:

B. Match the correct sums. (1 mark each)

/3

1. 5 + 2 •   • 6
2. 3 + 3 •   • 7
3. 7 + 1 •   • 8

C. Add the numbers. (2 marks each)

/14

1. 4 + 3 = ____
2. 2 + 9 = ____
3. 6 + 1 = ____
4. 3 + 2 = ____
5. $\begin{array}{r} 5 \\ +\ 8 \\ \hline \square \end{array}$
6. $\begin{array}{r} 7 \\ +\ 4 \\ \hline \square \end{array}$
7. $\begin{array}{r} 2 \\ +\ 6 \\ \hline \square \end{array}$

Total /20

BONUS

Find the sum of 4, 2, and 1.

____

Bonus /2

Test 6

- subtraction

A. Cross out the correct number of items. Then find the answer. (2 marks each)

8

1.

6 – 1 = ______

2.

7 – 2 = ______

3.

11 – 4 = ______

4.

12 – 7 = ______

Date:

B. Do the subtraction. Draw arrays to show your work. (2 marks each)

12

1. 10 – 4 = ____

2. 11 – 6 = ____

3. 15 – 9 = ____

4. 14 – 10 = ____

5.
$$\begin{array}{r} 13 \\ -\ 7 \\ \hline \square \end{array}$$

6.
$$\begin{array}{r} 9 \\ -\ 6 \\ \hline \square \end{array}$$

Total

20

Math

Test 7

- **addition and subtraction**

A. Add or subtract with the help of the pictures. (1 mark each)

___ / 8

1. $3 + 2 = \square$

2. $5 + 1 = \square$

3. $7 - 4 = \square$

4. $6 - 3 = \square$

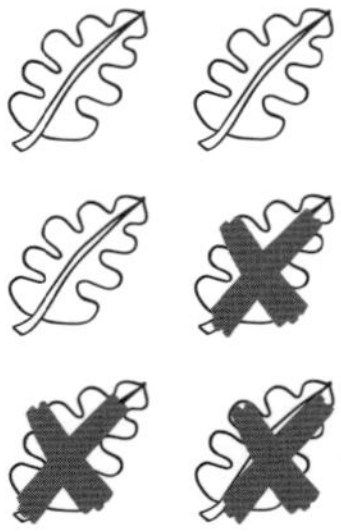

5. $2 + 5 = \square$

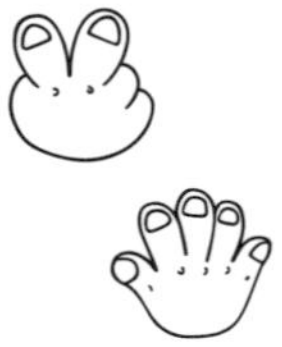

6. $8 - 3 = \square$

Date:

7. 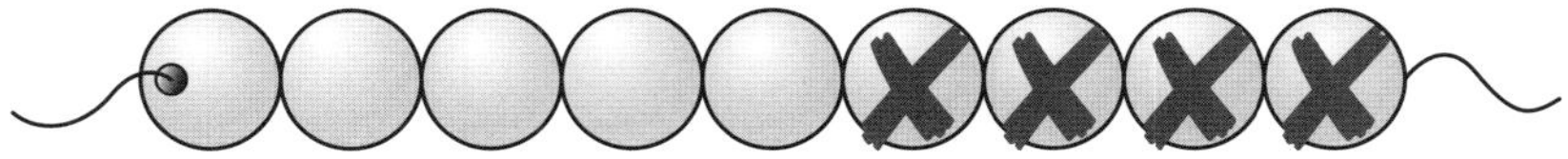

9 – 4 = ____

8. 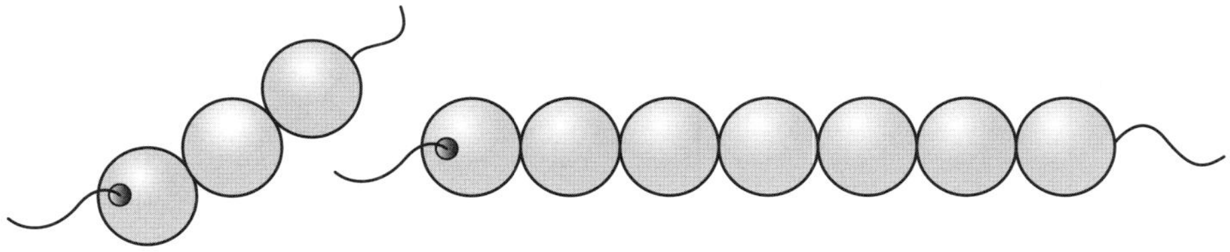

3 + 7 = ____

B. Add or subtract. (2 marks each)

12

1.
$$\begin{array}{r} 4 \\ +\ 6 \\ \hline \square \end{array}$$

2.
$$\begin{array}{r} 11 \\ -\ 6 \\ \hline \square \end{array}$$

3. 10 – 3 = ____

4. 5 + 4 = ____

5. 3 + 9 = ____

6. 12 – 2 = ____

Total

20

Test 8

- money

A. Write the total value of each group of coins. (2 marks each)

/4

1.

______ cents

2.

______ cents

B. Check the correct coins to show the value of each item. (2 marks each)

/4

1.

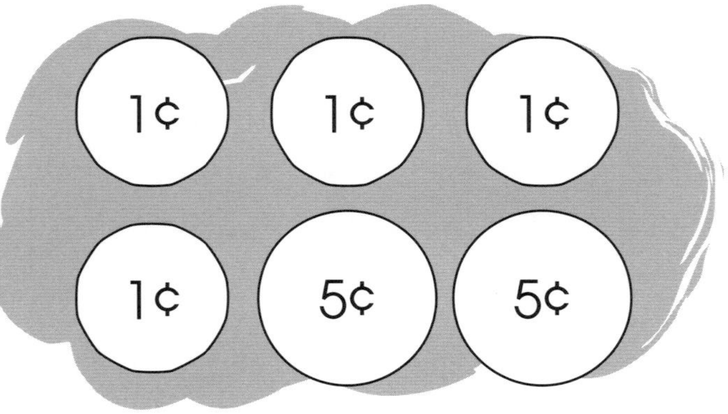

2.

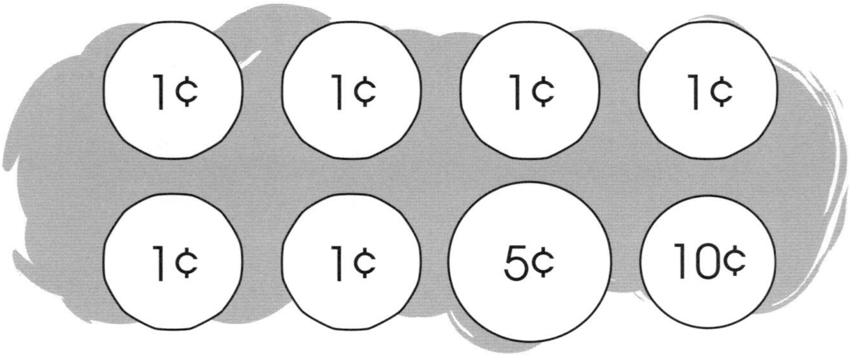

C. Draw the fewest coins to show each value.

(3 marks each)

12

= 10¢

= 5¢

= 1¢

1. **6** cents

2. **13** cents

3. **16** cents

4. **15** cents

Total

20

Test 9

- time

A. Check the correct time. (1 mark each)

2

1.

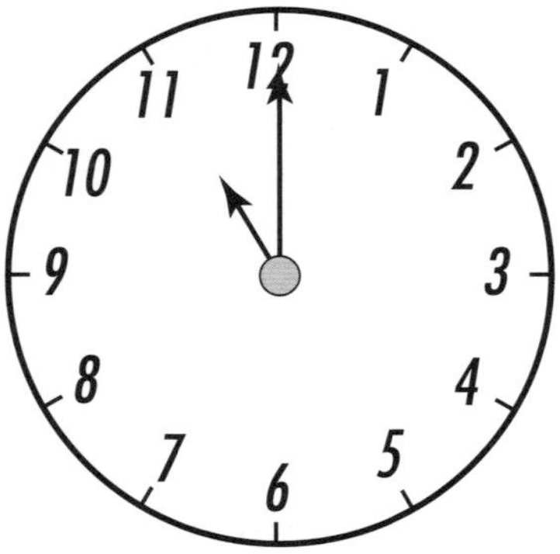

Ⓐ 3 o'clock

Ⓑ 11 o'clock

2.

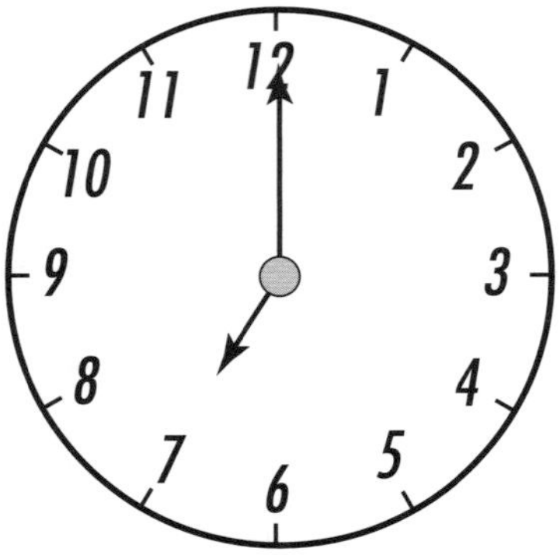

Ⓐ 7 o'clock

Ⓑ 8 o'clock

B. Write the time and fill in the blanks with the given words. (4 marks each)

8

1.

_____ o'clock

____

morning / afternoon / night

2.

_____ o'clock

____

morning / afternoon / night

Date:

C. Draw the clock hands. (2 marks each)

10

1. **1 o'clock**

2. **5 o'clock**

3. **9 o'clock**

4. **6 o'clock**

5. **4 o'clock**

Total

20

Math

Test 10

- **days of the week**

A. Fill in the missing letters to complete the days of the week. (1 mark each)

7

B. Write the days. (1 mark each)

3

1. The first day of the week: ____________
2. The day that comes after Monday: ____________
3. The day that comes before Thursday: ____________

C. Read Judy's notes and complete her plan. Then fill in the blanks. (2 marks each)

10

Notes

I will visit Grandma  *on the day after Saturday. I will stay with her for two days. Then I will be back home* *. On the day before Friday, I will go to see the dentist* 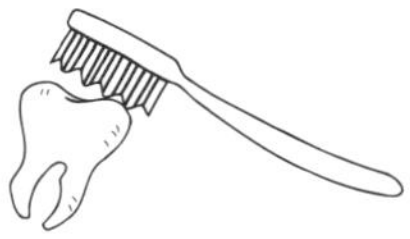 *.*

Judy's Plan

Sun
Mon
Tue
Wed
Thu
Fri
Sat

- Judy will go to a birthday party on the day after Tuesday. The party is on

  ________________ .

- Judy wants to go camping for two days. On which days should she go camping?

  ____

Total

20

Test 11

- temperature

Math

A. Name each season. Then write the order of the seasons. Start with 1 for spring.
(3 marks each)

12

Order of the Seasons

1. 

2. 

3. 

4. 

Date:

B. Check the ones that describe each season.
(2 marks each)

8

1. **Fall**
   - (A) hot
   - (B) getting colder
   - (C) leaves falling

2. **Summer**
   - (A) hot
   - (B) humid
   - (C) leaves turning yellow

3. **Winter**
   - (A) cold
   - (B) snow
   - (C) bees buzzing

4. **Spring**
   - (A) cold
   - (B) snow melting
   - (C) flowers blossoming

BONUS

Name the season that the objects belong to.

Total
20

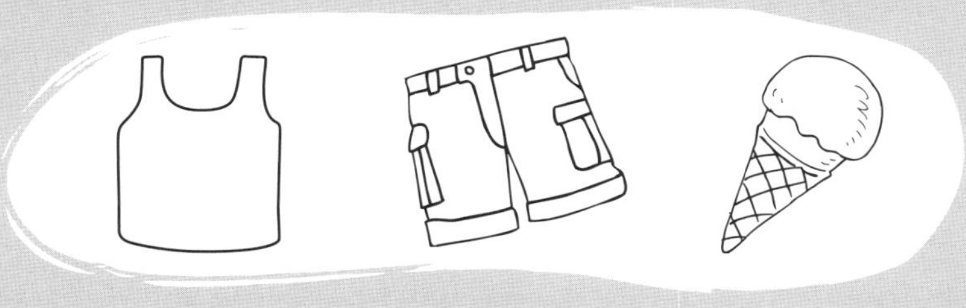

Bonus
/ 2

Season

Test 12

- ordinal numbers

A. Write the ordinal numbers. (1 mark each)

4

1. 4th

____

2. 9th

____

3. 10th

____

4. 1st

____

B. Write the order of the animals with ordinal numbers. (2 marks each)

10

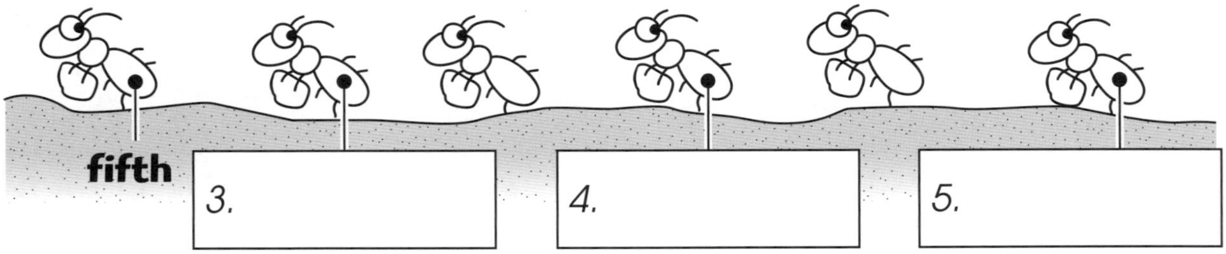

C. Draw the children and put their names in the boxes. (2 marks each)

6

1. Sue  is the second person in line.
2. Josh  is the fifth person in line.
3. Kelvin is the third person in line.

Total 20

BONUS

Write the ordinal numbers that come after second and before fifth.

____

Bonus /2

Test 13

- comparing different lengths

Math

A. Look at the items below. Circle the "longer" or "shorter" item. (2 marks each)

12

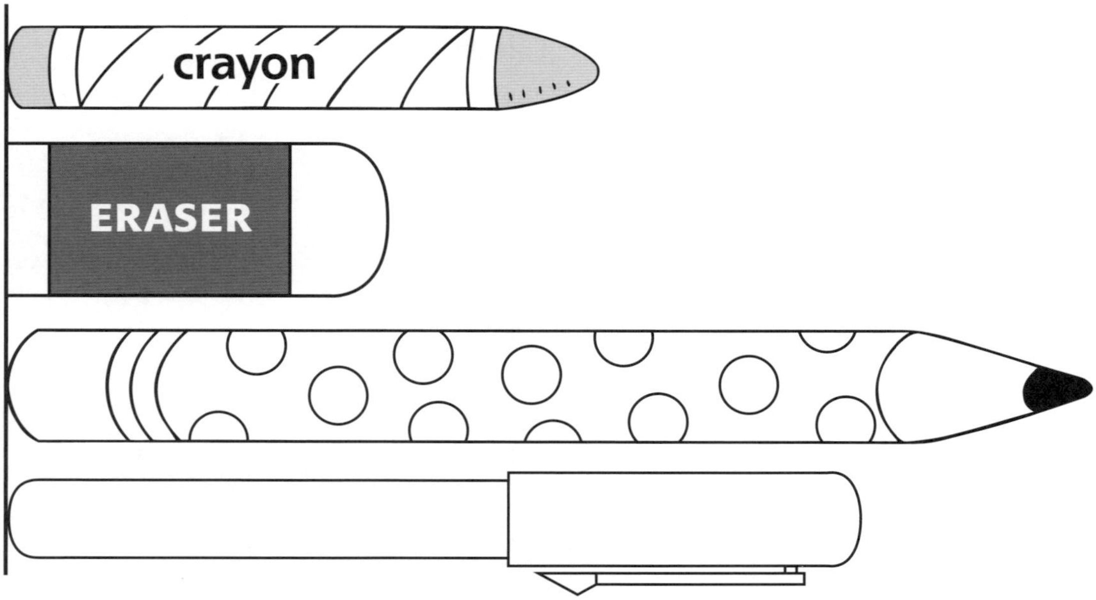

1. longer

   crayon pencil

2. shorter

   eraser crayon

3. shorter

   pen eraser

4. longer

   crayon pen

5. longer

   pencil eraser

6. shorter

   pen pencil

B. Which object is taller or shorter? Fill in the blanks. (2 marks each)

8

1. The house is ______________ than the tree.

2. The boy is ______________ than the girl.

3. The ______________ is taller than the tree.

4. The ______________ is taller than the house but shorter than the building.

Total

20

Test 14

- **comparing different lengths**

Math

A. Colour the ribbons. Then answer the questions. (2 marks each)

8

1. Colour the longest ribbon red and the shortest one green.
2. Draw a ribbon in the box that is a bit longer than the dotted ribbon but shorter than the striped one.
3. Put the ribbons in order from longest to shortest. Write 1 to 4 in the circles. 1 is the longest.
4. There are _____ ribbons that are shorter than the ribbon with stripes.

Order
(longest → shortest)

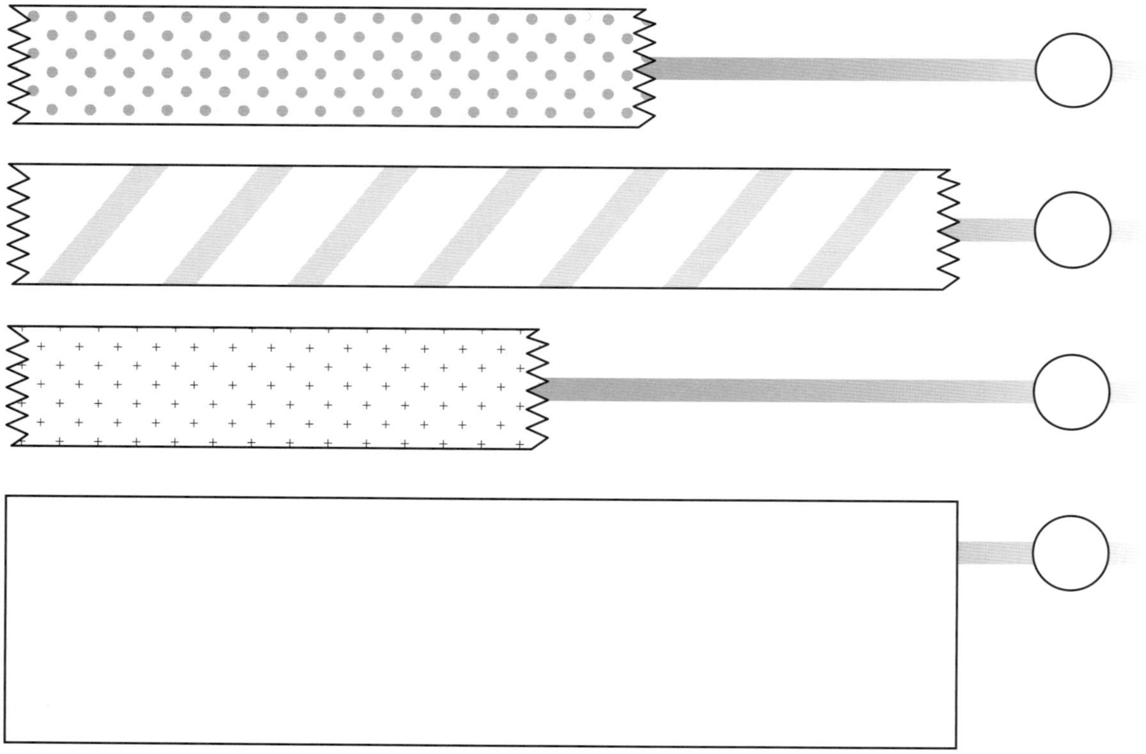

B. Find the answers. (3 marks each)

12

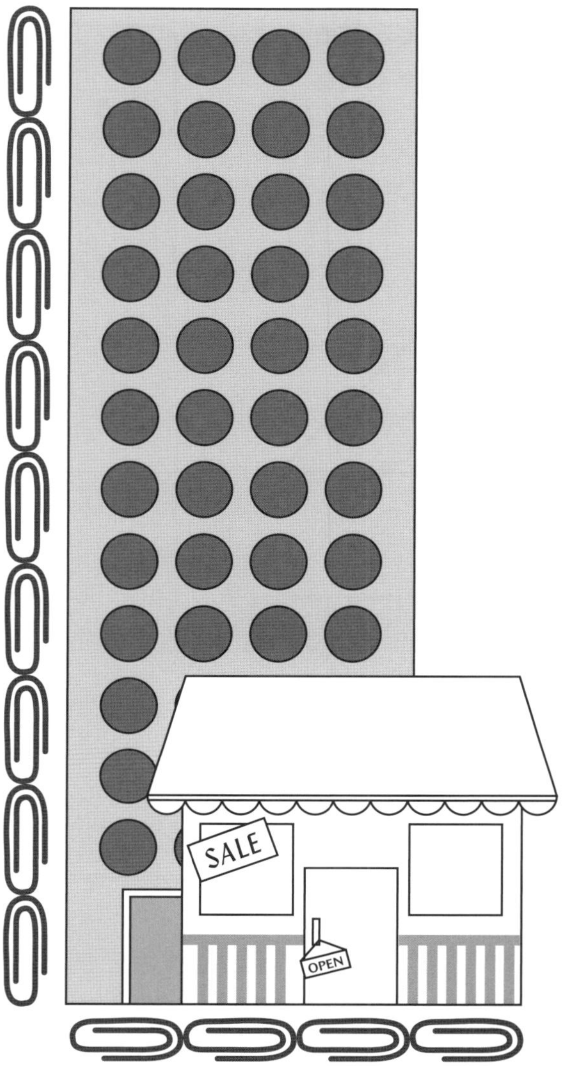

1. Building

   height: ______ 📎

   width: ______ 📎

2. Shop

   height: ______ 📎

   width: ______ 📎

3. The building is ______ 📎 taller than the shop.

4. The width of the shop and the building is ________________ .
   the same / different

Total
20

BONUS

A factory is 4 📎 tall and 3 📎 wide. Is the factory larger or smaller than the shop above?

____

Bonus
/ 2

Test 15

- area

Math

A. Record the area of the shapes that are measured in different units. Circle the one that has the greatest area. (4 marks each)

8

1.

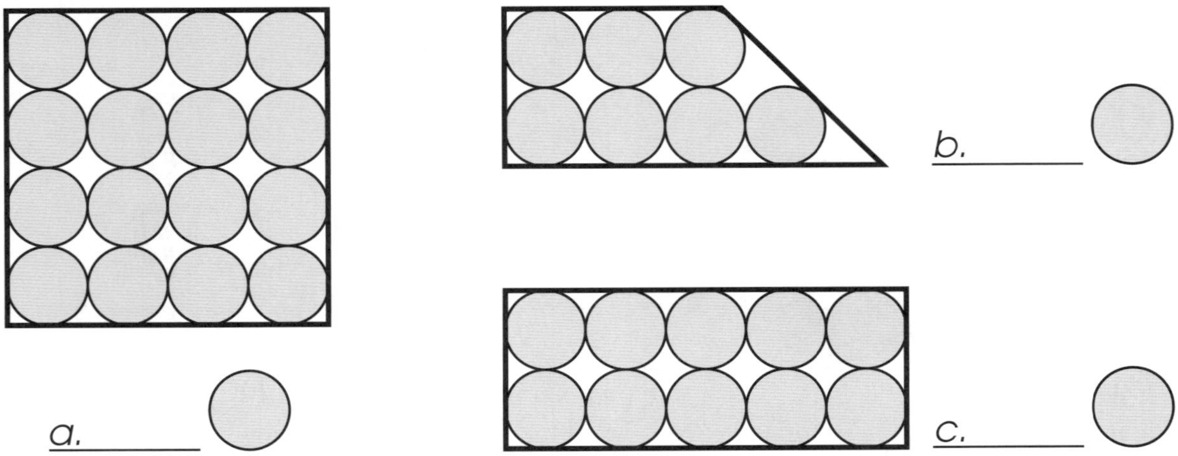

2.

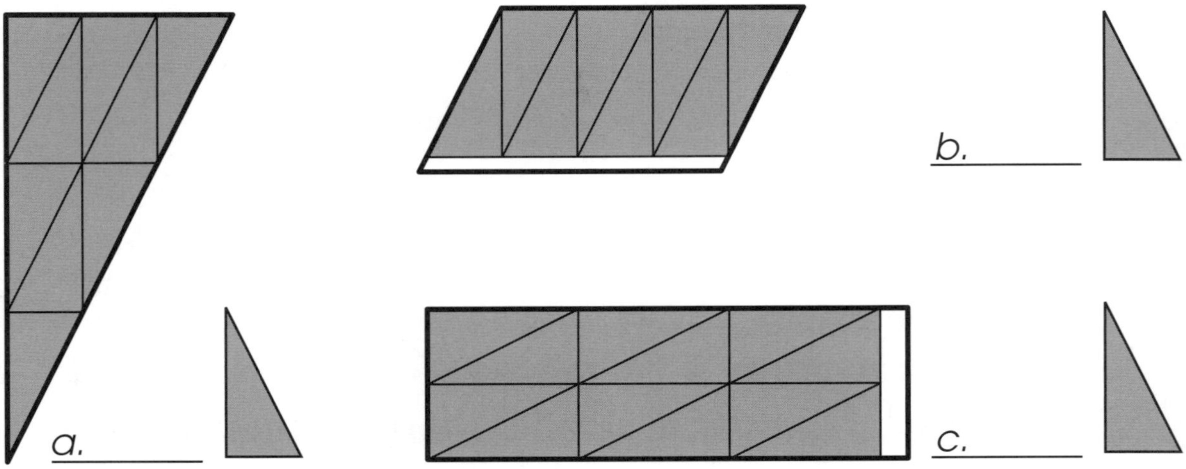

B. Find the area of the pictures. Then answer the questions. (3 marks each)

12

A

B

C

1. **AREA**

A: ____ ☐

B: ____ ☐

C: ____ ☐

2. Picture ____ has the largest area.

3. Picture ____ has the smallest area.

4. Picture B is ____ ☐ larger than picture C.

Total

20

Test 16

- capacity

A. Circle the container that has a greater capacity than the one in the circle. (2 marks each)

8

1.

2.

3.

4.

B. Estimate how many small containers are needed to have capacities equal to each big container. Circle the reasonable answer. (2 marks each)

12

1.

2
16

2.

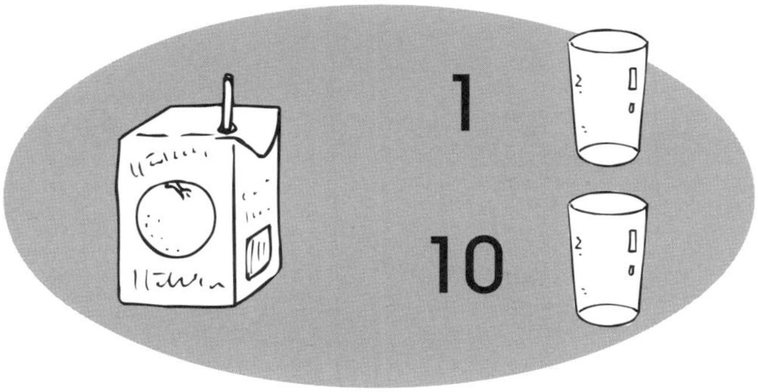

1
10

3.

6
40

4.

3
20

5.

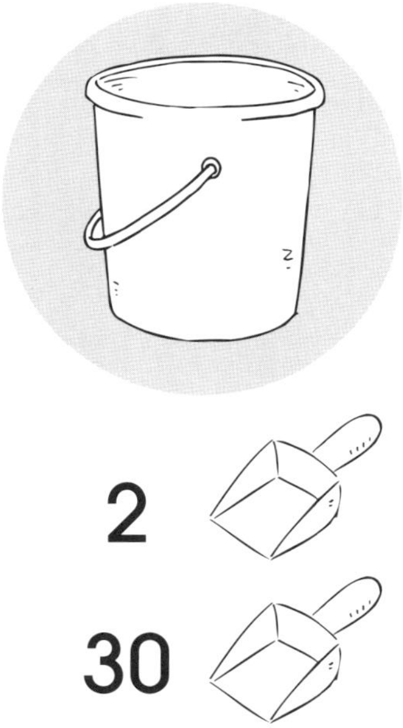

2
30

6.

5
80

Total

20

Test 17

- mass

A. Circle the heavier object in each group.

(2 marks each) 6

1.

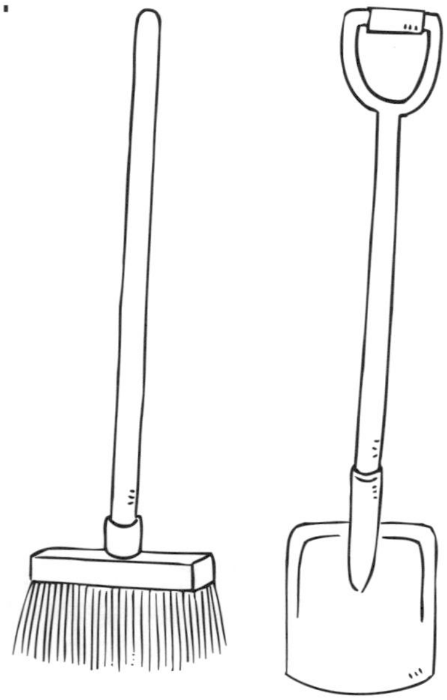

2.

3.

B. Put the objects in order from lightest to heaviest. Write 1 to 3. (3 marks each)

6

1.

2.

C. Choose the object that makes each picture true. Write the letter in the circle. (2 marks each)

8

1.

2.

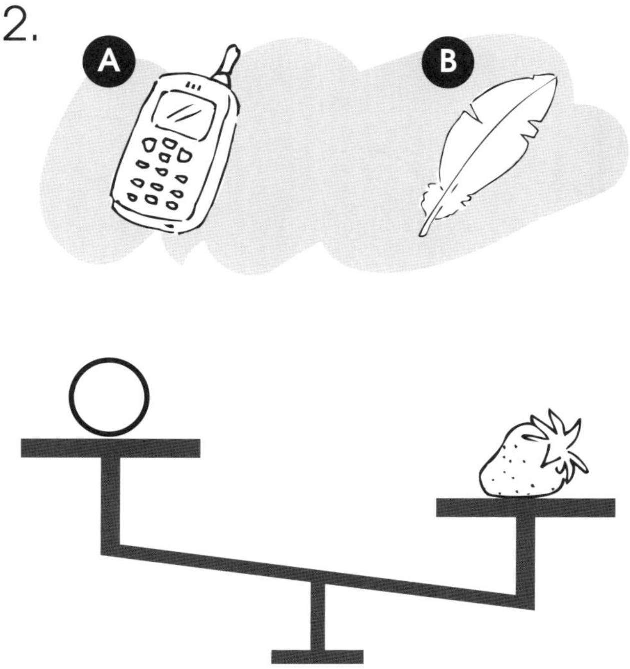

3.

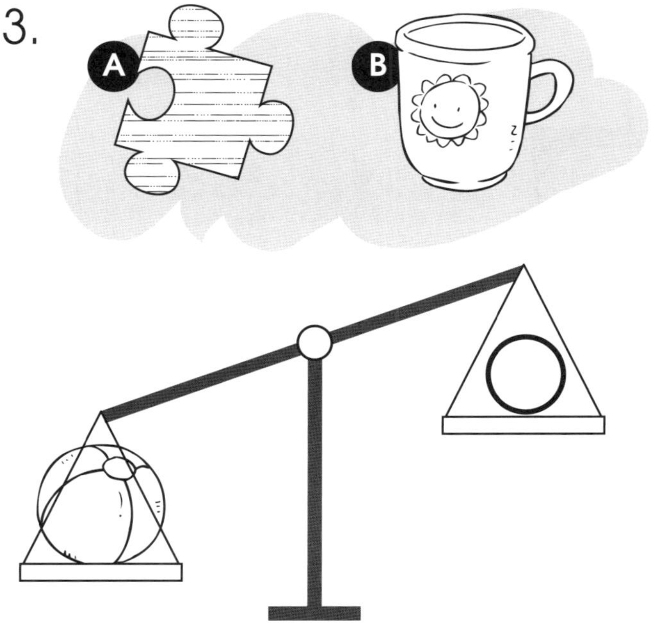

4.

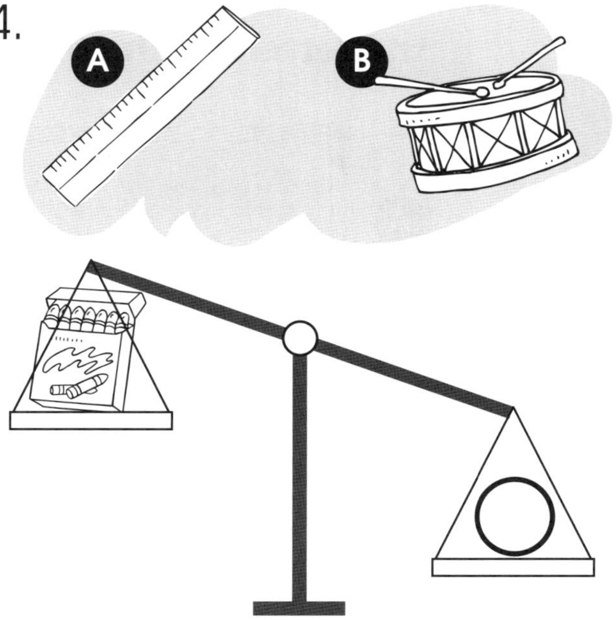

Total

20

Test 18

- shapes

A. Cross out the shape that does not belong in each group. (1 mark each)

2

1.

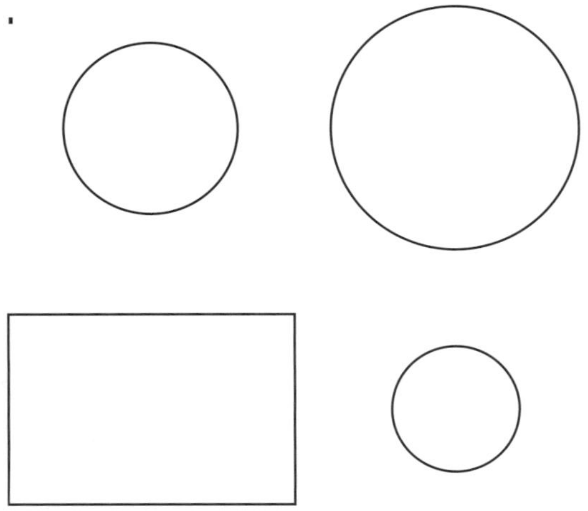

2.

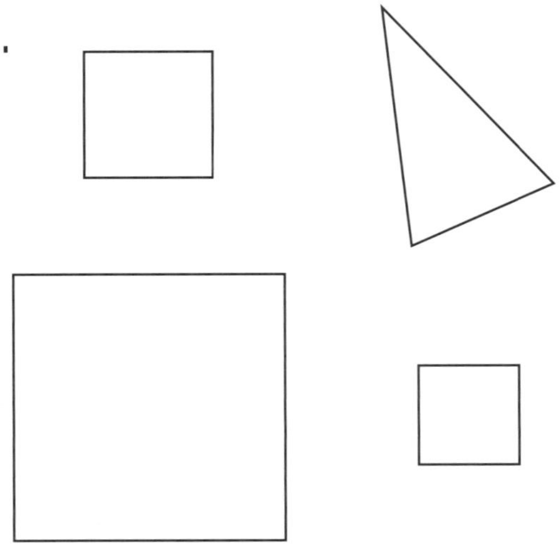

B. Match the shape with each object. Write the letter on the line. (1 mark each)

6

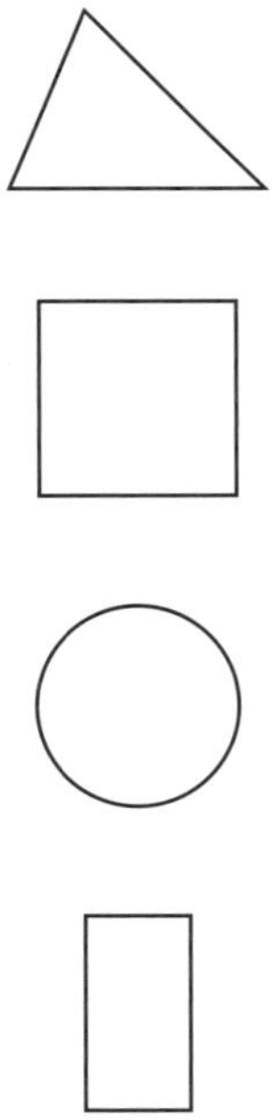

C. Write the number of sides that each shape has.

(2 marks each)

12

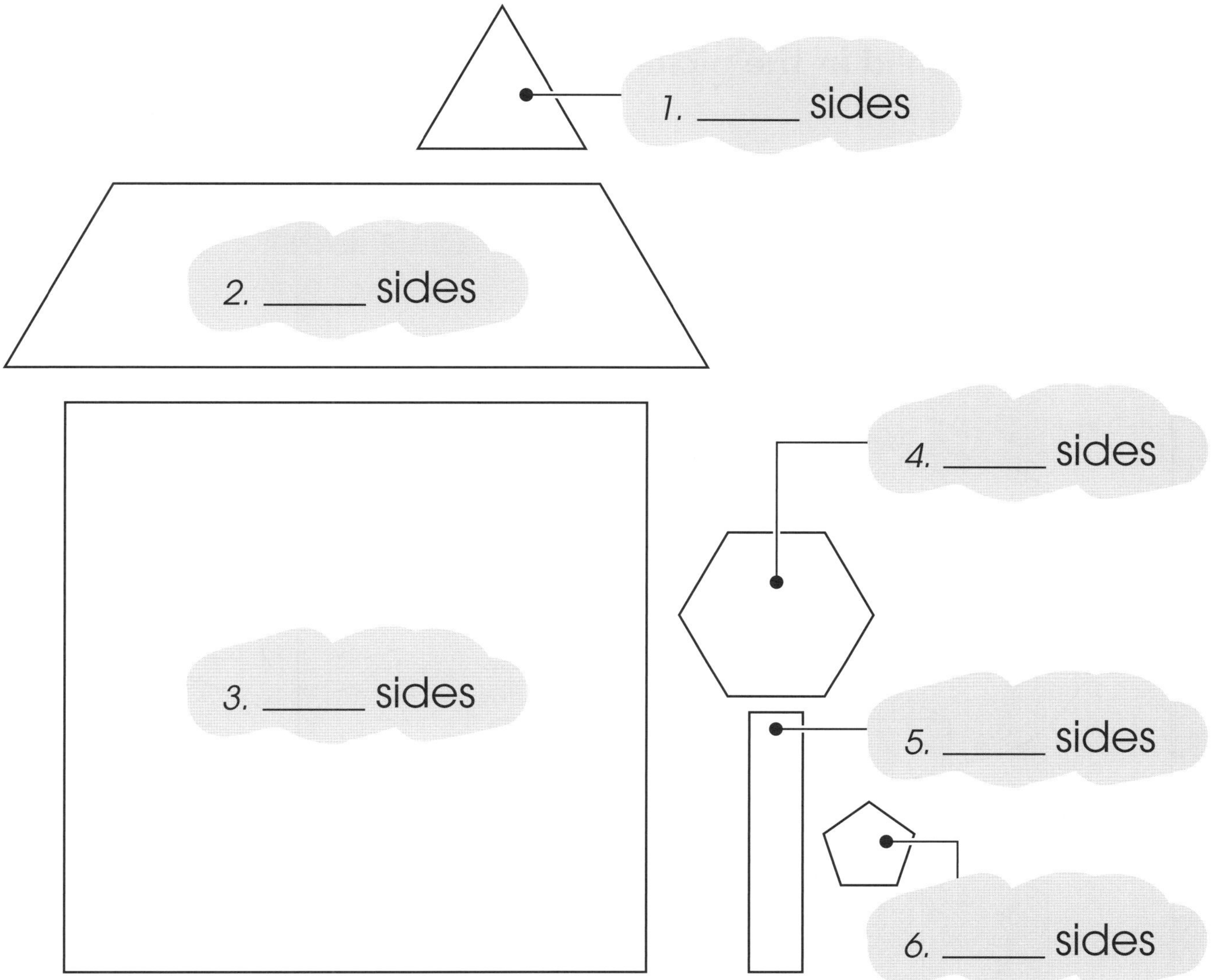

1. ______ sides

2. ______ sides

3. ______ sides

4. ______ sides

5. ______ sides

6. ______ sides

Total

20

BONUS

"Hex" means "six" in Greek. Check the shape below that is a hexagon (has 6 sides).

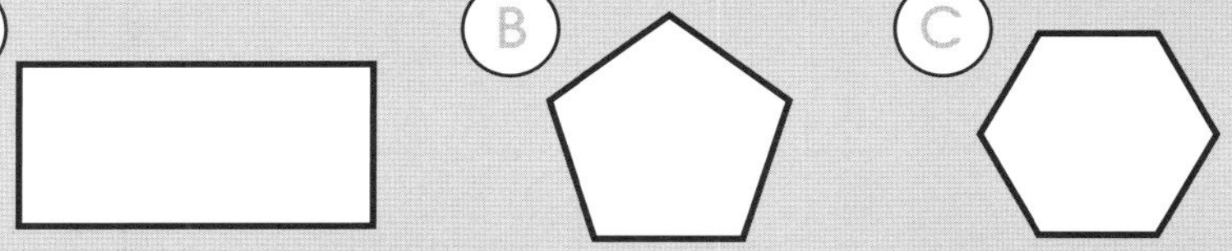

A B C

Bonus

/2

Test 19

Math

- solids

A. Name the solids and count the number of each solid in the picture. (2 marks each)

10

Sphere Cone Cylinder Rectangular Prism Cube

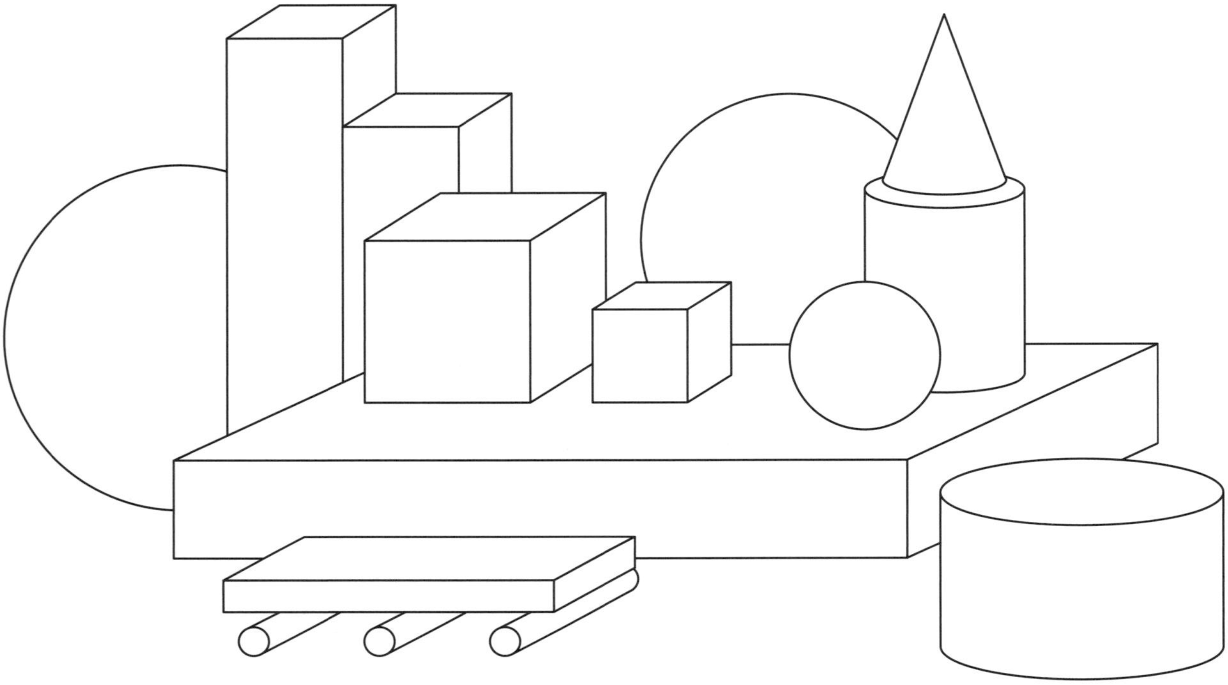

		Name of Solid	Number of Solid
1.	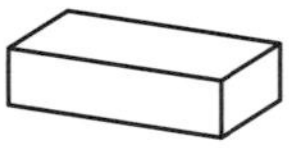	____________	______
2.	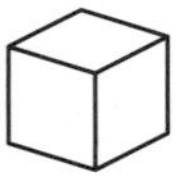	____________	______
3.	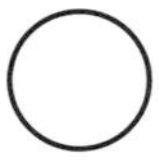	____________	______
4.		____________	______
5.		____________	______

B. Colour the correct solid(s). (2 marks each)

10

1. can roll

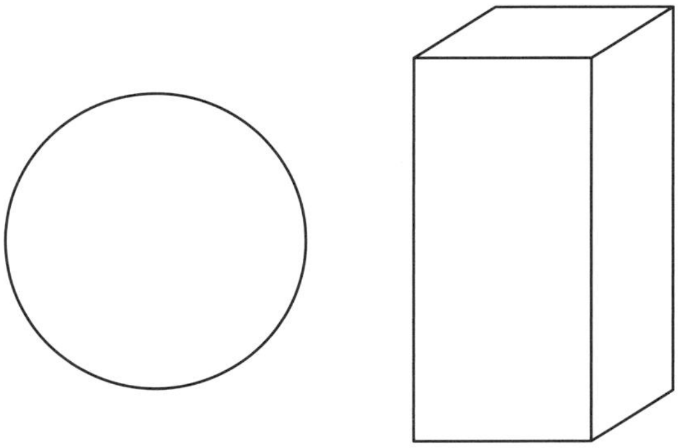

2. can be stacked

3. have corners

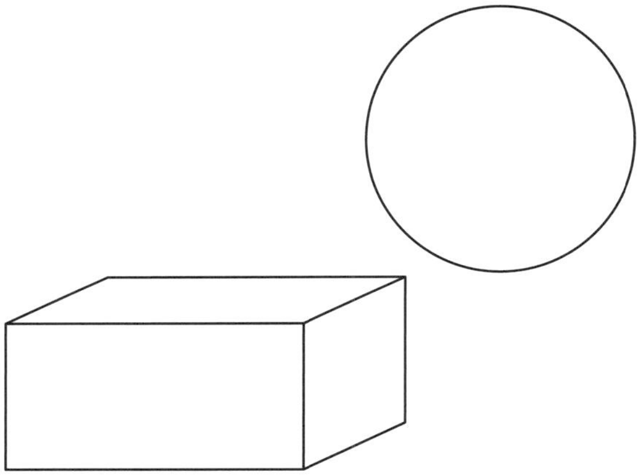

4. have circular faces

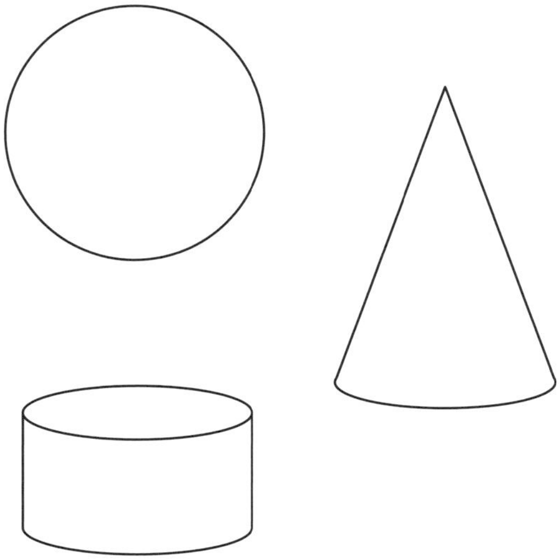

5. have rectangular faces

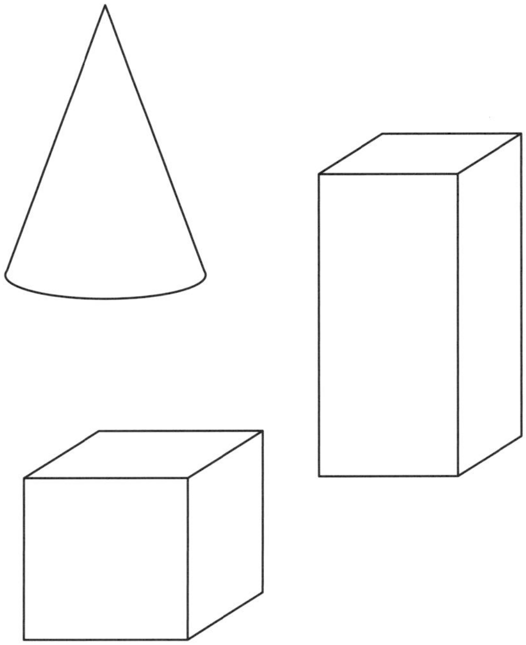

Test 20

- symmetry

Math

A. Check the pictures that are divided into halves and put a cross for the ones that are not. (2 marks each)

8

1.

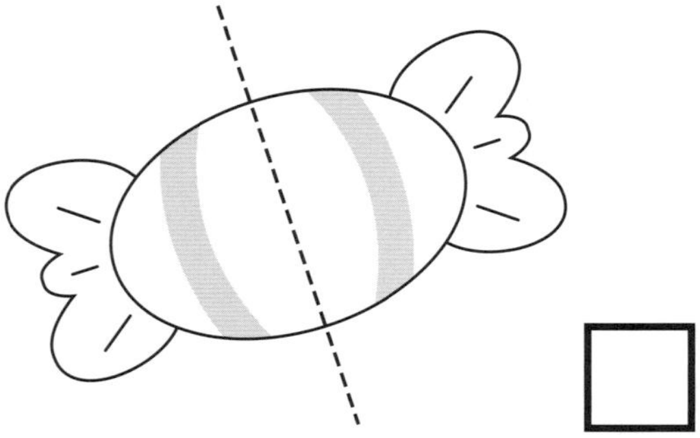

2.

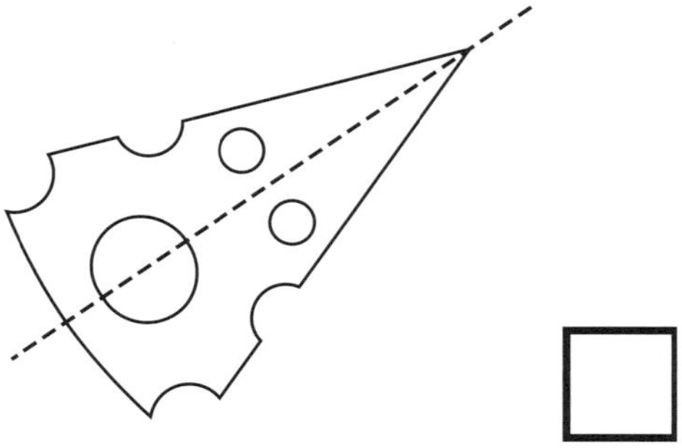

3.

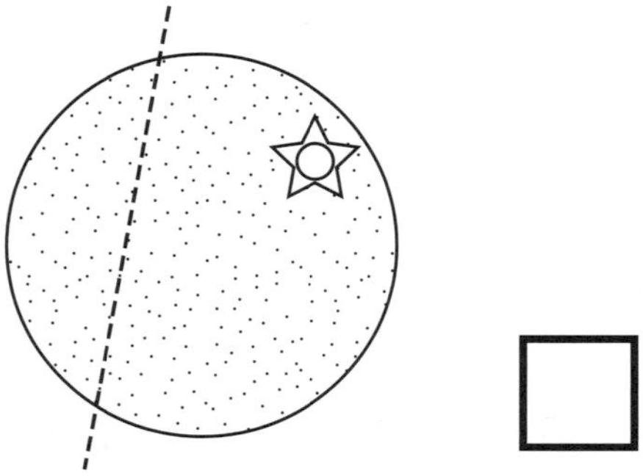

4.

B. Draw a line through each picture to show two equal parts. (2 marks each)

4

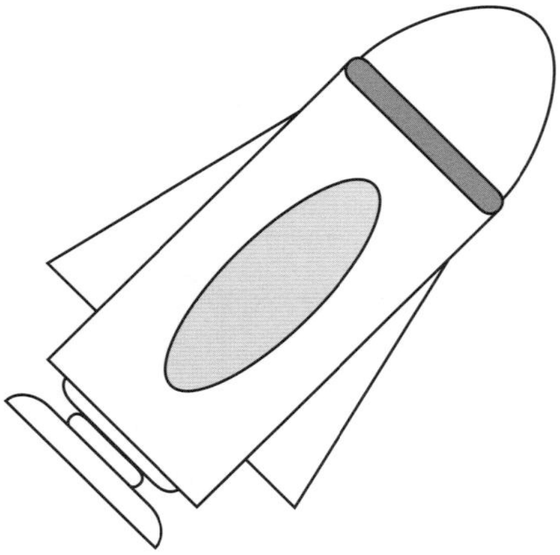

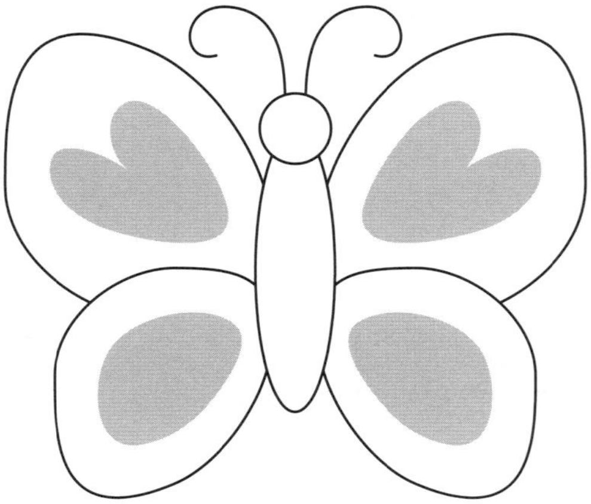

C. Draw matching parts to complete each picture.

(2 marks each)

8

1.

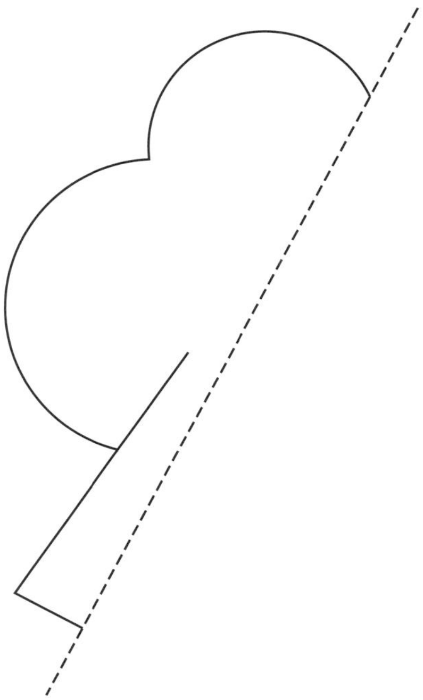

2.

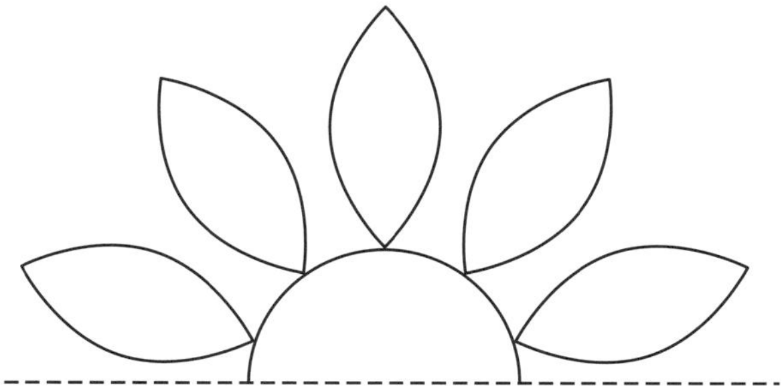

3.

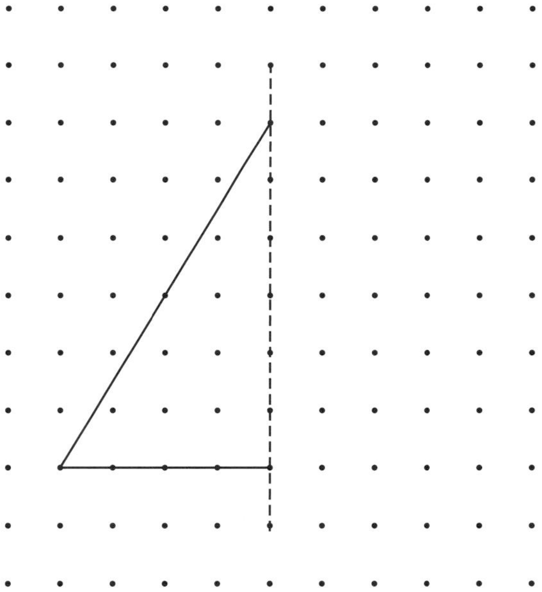

4.

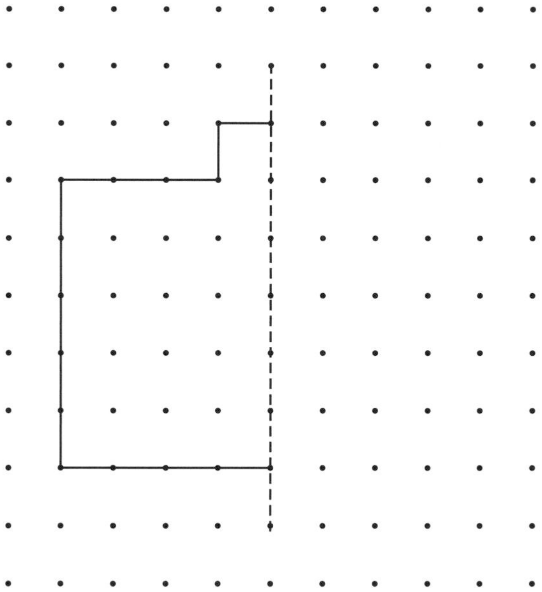

Total

20

Test 21

• **location of objects**

Math

A. Look at the picture. Check the word that completes each sentence. (2 marks each)

8

1. 

The toy car is ______ the box.

(A) under (B) in front of

2. 

The doll is holding a lollipop in her ______ hand.

(A) right (B) left

3. 

The shoes are ______ the box.

(A) inside (B) under

4. 

The butterfly is flying ______ the flowers.

(A) over (B) behind

B. Look at the picture. Complete the sentences with the given words. (2 marks each)

12

over
under
on
in
left
right
beside
in front of
behind

1. There is a box ____________ the girl.
2. The ball is ____________ the box.
3. The puppy is sitting ____________ the carpet.
4. A spider is hanging ____________ the toy car.
5. The toy car is ____________ the puppy.
6. The carpet is ____________ the box.

Total

20

Test 22

- **number patterns**

A. Follow the pattern to draw the beads. Then complete the number patterns. (4 marks each)

8

1.

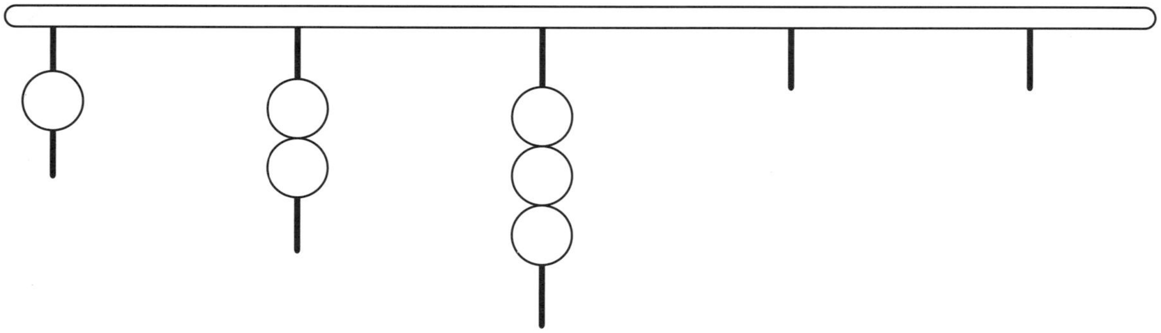

Number Pattern

1 2 3 ______ ______

2.

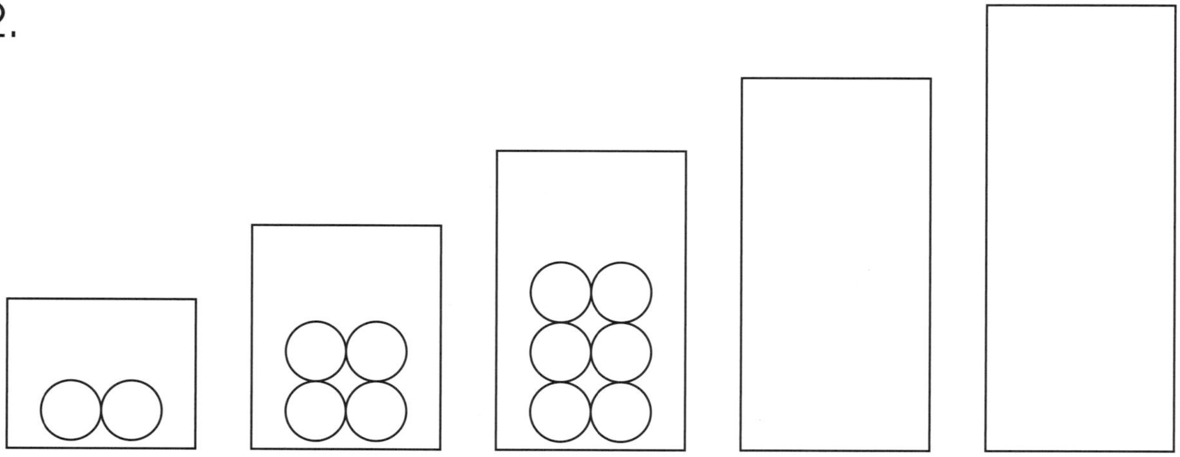

Number Pattern

2 4 6 ______ ______

Date:

B. Fill in the blanks with the given choices. Then complete the patterns. (3 marks each)

12

1. Count by ________ .
   1's / 2's

   2, 4, 6, ______, ______

2. Count by ________ .
   1's / 10's

   1, 2, 3, ______, ______

3. Count by ________ .
   2's / 10's

   10, 20, 30, ______, ______

4. Count by ________ .
   5's / 10's

   5, 10, 15, ______, ______

Total
20

BONUS

Check the next number in the pattern.

Pattern
10, 8, 6, 4, ?

Ⓐ 1 Ⓑ 2 Ⓒ 3

Bonus
/2

Test 23

Math

- patterning with shapes

A. Circle the correct word to describe the pattern change. Then draw the shape that comes next. (4 marks each)

___ / 8

1.

Pattern change: size / orientation / shape

2.

Pattern change: size / orientation / shape

B. Create a pattern that changes in shape. (4 marks)

___ / 4

C. Describe the patterns with the given words. Then draw the one that comes next. (4 marks each)

8

growing **shrinking** **repeating**

1.

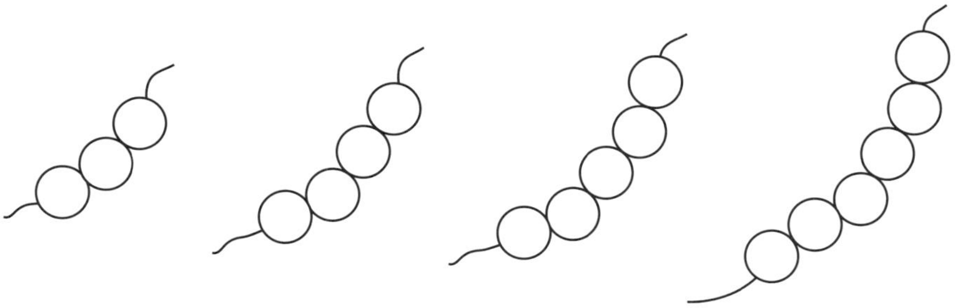

It is a ______________ pattern.

2.

It is a ______________ pattern.

Total 20

BONUS

Check the next picture.

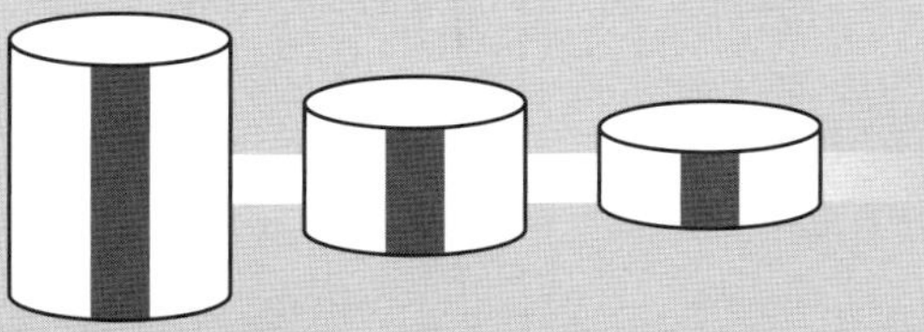

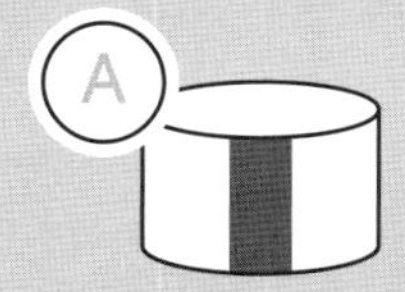

Bonus /2

Test 24

- sorting

A. Cross out the object that does not belong in each group. (2 marks each)

4

1\.

2\.

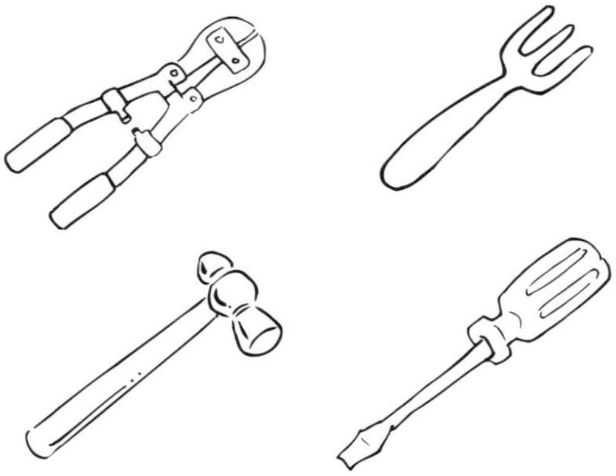

B. Cross out the object that does not belong in the group. Then draw lines to match the group with the correct objects. (2 marks each)

8

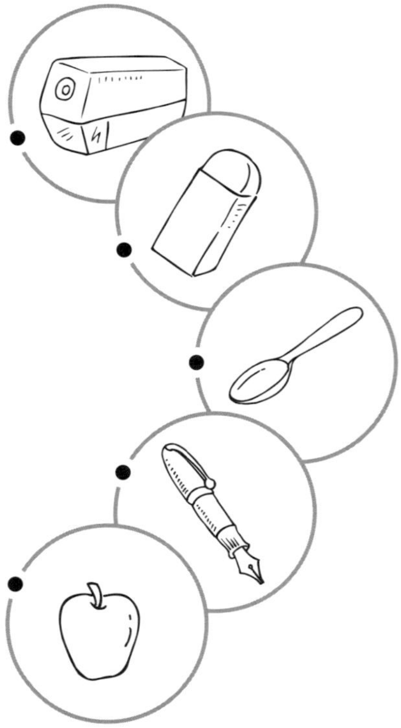

C. Draw an object that belongs to each group.

(2 marks each)

8

1.

2.

3.

4.

BONUS

Name the groups.

Groups ____________

____________ **and** ____________

Total

20

Bonus

/ 2

Test 25

- pictograph

A. Look at the pictograph. Complete the chart.

(4 marks)

/4

Our Favourite Juice

Juice	Number of Children
orange	
apple	
mango	
grape	

B. Answer the questions using the pictograph in (A). (2 marks each)

/8

1. Which is the most popular flavour? ____________

2. Which is the least popular flavour? ____________

3. How many more children like apple juice than mango juice? ____________

4. How many children voted? ____________

C. Colour the pictograph to show the number of each kind of bead on the necklace. Then complete the sentences. (2 marks each)

8

1. **Number of Beads**

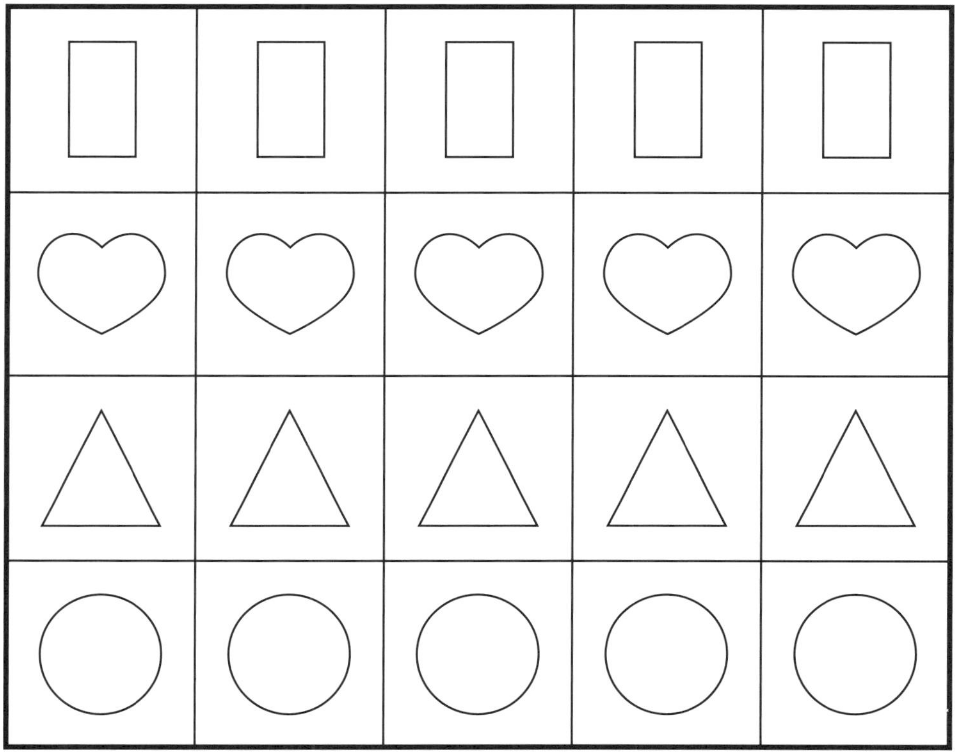

2. There are ☐ kinds of beads.

3. There are ☐ more △ than ♡ .

4. ☐ is the most used shape of bead.

Total

20

Test 26

- **probability**

Math

A. Match the word that best describes the likelihood of each event. (2 marks each)

8

1. certain •
2. likely •
3. unlikely •
4. impossible •

- •
- • Jack breathes every day.
- • Jack drank some water yesterday.
- • Jack will eat 10 apples for breakfast tomorrow

B. Check the correct answers. (2 marks each)

4

1. The puppy's heart beats.

   (A) certain (B) unlikely (C) impossible

2. The teddy bear will turn into a robot tomorrow.

   (A) certain (B) unlikely (C) impossible

C. Look at the spinner and write the correct word to describe each event. (2 marks each)

8

certain impossible likely unlikely

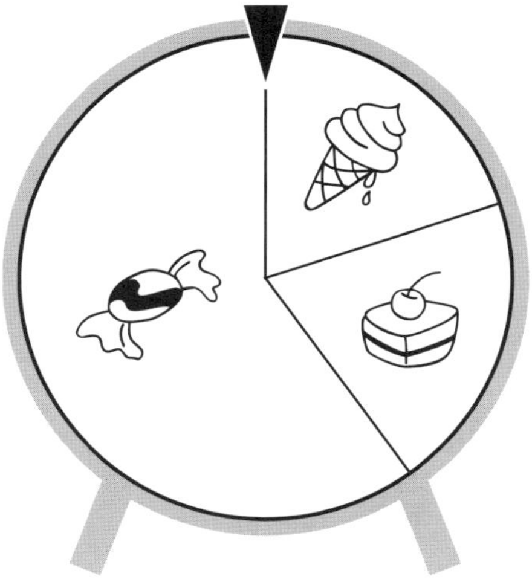

1. The spinner lands on  .

____

2. The spinner lands on  .

____

3. The spinner lands on  .

____

4. The spinner lands on , , or  .

____

Total

20

BONUS

Draw  and  on the spinner.

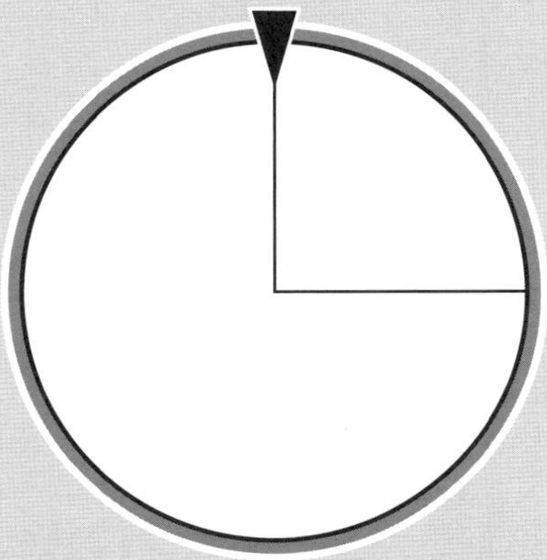

The probability of spinning

-  is likely.
-  is unlikely.

Bonus

/2

Math

My Test Record

Test 1

- numbers and number words

____ / 20

Test 2

- more or less

____ / 20

Test 3

- more than 5

____ / 20

Test 4

- less than 10

____ / 20

Test 5

- addition

____ / 20

Test 6

- subtraction

____ / 20

Test 7

- addition and subtraction

____ / 20

Test 8

- money

____ / 20

Test 9

- time

____ / 20

Test 10

- days of the week

____ / 20

Test 11

- temperature

____ / 20

Test 12

- ordinal numbers

____ / 20

Test 13

- comparing different lengths

/20

Test 14

- comparing different lengths

/20

Test 15

- area

/20

Test 16

- capacity

/20

Test 17

- mass

/20

Test 18

- shapes

/20

Test 19

- solids

/20

Test 20

- symmetry

/20

Test 21

- location of objects

/20

Test 22

- number patterns

/20

Test 23

- patterning with shapes

/20

Test 24

- sorting

/20

Test 25

- pictograph

/20

Test 26

- probability

/20

TestSmart

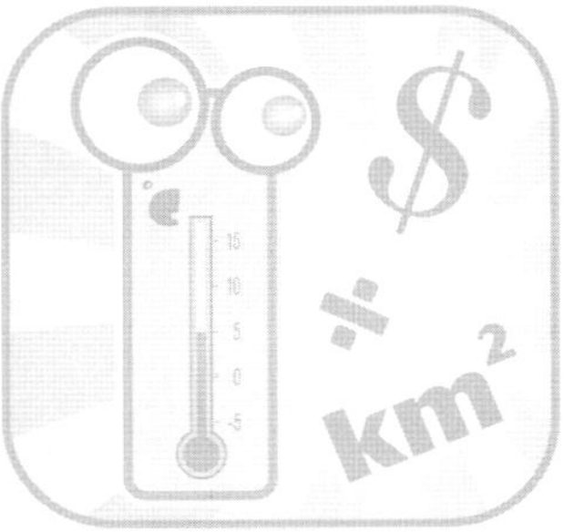

Social Studies

Test 1

- **responsibilities**
- **rules**

A. Check the sentence that describes a child's responsible action. Then decide who benefits most from this action. Write "child", "family", or "both" in the box. (4 marks each)

16

1. (A) I help my little brother read his book.
   (B) I have a muffin for breakfast.

2. (A) I am late for school.
   (B) I brush my teeth morning and night.

3. (A) I take the garbage to the outside bin.
   (B) I turn on the TV.

4. (A) I like my dog.
   (B) I play with my dog every day.

B. Read the rules that the children know. Choose the correct new rule for each change. (2 marks each)

4

1.

I only practise biking in the backyard.

What if Mom comes with me?

(A) Mom rides my bike.

(B) I ride my bike to the park.

2.

I always use my indoor voice at the library.

What if there is an emergency?

(A) I use my outdoor voice.

(B) I whisper.

Total

20

BONUS

Answer the question.

Can you think of one rule that changes as you get older?

____

Bonus

/2

Test 2

- **rules, responsibilities, and relationships**

A. Check the correct answer to complete the sentence. Then decide whether "Rules" or "Responsibilities" help build a relationship in each. (4 marks each)

12

1. If you walk your dog every day, it will

   (A) get very tired.

   (B) become one of your best friends.

   ______________________ help build a relationship.

2. If you follow the sign in the park and keep your dog on its leash, you will make sure that

   (A) your dog does not chase people or animals.

   (B) your dog gets tangled in park benches.

   ______________________ help build a relationship.

3. If you empty the garbage, your mom

   (A) will have a bit more free time.

   (B) will be upset because she wanted to do it.

   ______________________ help build a relationship.

B. Choose the best word(s) for each and write it on the line. (2 marks each)

8

relationship **responsibility**
rule **bigger responsibility**

1. *I just got a puppy, and it's my job to feed it every day.*

____

2. Ben makes sure he feeds his puppy a cup of kibble twice a day, just like the vet said. ______________

3. Ben's parents are proud that Ben has been so good about feeding the puppy. ______________

4. Ben's parents decide that Ben is ready to start taking his puppy for a walk every day.

____

Total

20

Test 3

- types of community
- community needs

A. Identify the type of community each picture shows and write it in the box. Then match the other words to each community. (4 marks each)

12

rural community	tractor repair shops	malls	barns
farm community	skyscrapers	lakes	highways
big city	canoe rental shops	fields	rocky

1.

2.

3.

B. Every community has services for the needs of its members. Read each sentence and circle which community service is needed. (2 marks each)

8

1. 

dentist / police officer / doctor

2. Henry would like to read a new book.

grocery store / library / hospital

3. Ella wants to mail a letter.

post box / police station / pool

4. Sammi and Jack are hungry.

school / community centre / restaurant

Total

20

Test 4

- travelling in a community
- community signs

A. Describe how each person is travelling. Then answer the question. (2 marks each)

12

1.

2.

3.

4.

Which two ways can you travel and get exercise?

5. ________________ and 6. ________________

B. Circle the correct answers. (2 marks each)

8

1. Signs often show people / rules / animals we should follow.

2. Obeying signs when we travel helps keep us on time / healthy / safe .

3. Which sign means "No Biking"?

4. Which sign means it is safe to walk across the street?

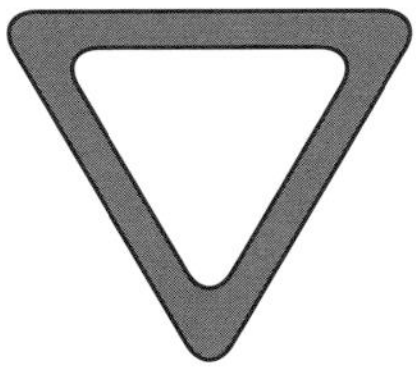

Total

20

Test 5

- different jobs in a community

A. Name the jobs in a community. Then match the pictures with the workers by writing the letters on the lines. (3 marks each)

15

Jobs

- teacher
- zoo keeper
- librarian
- farmer
- police officer
- mail carrier
- baker
- construction worker

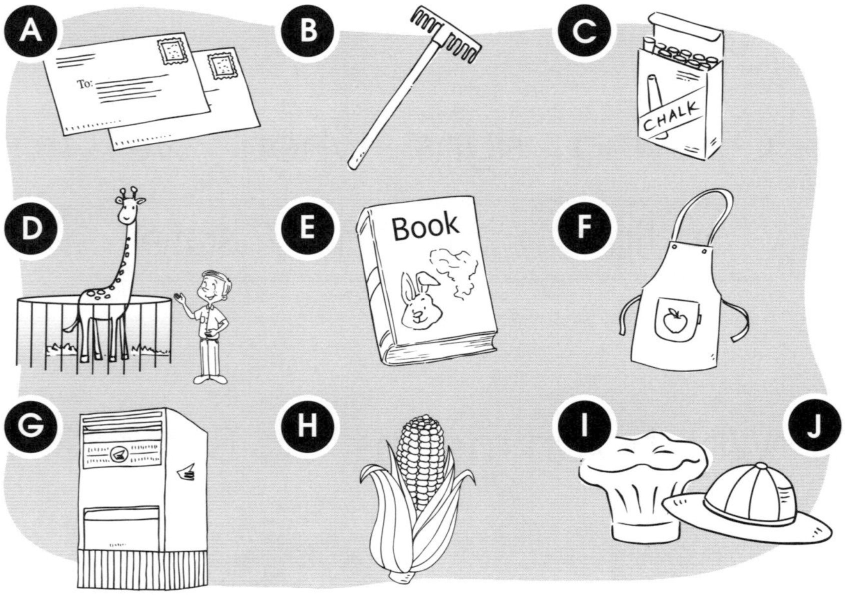

1. ______________________
   - feeds zoo animals
   - ______ and ______

2. ______________________
   - writes on a blackboard
   - ______ and ______

3. ______________________
   - grows corn
   - ______ and ______

4. ______________________
   - bakes sweet treats
   - ______ and ______

5. ______________________
   - delivers letters
   - ______ and ______

B. Write whether the thing is a "tool" or a "product". Then answer the question. (1 mark each)

5

5. What job does this person have?

____

Total

20

Answer the questions.

Where do apples come from? Who grows them?

____

____

Bonus

/ 2

Test 6

- safety workers
- health workers

A. Check the two safety workers. Then fill in the blanks to complete the sentences that describe the safety workers. (4 marks each)

12

1. **Safety Workers**

(A) teachers
(B) firefighters
(C) mail carriers
(D) landscapers
(E) police officers
(F) caretakers

2. ____________________ travel in special cars with red and blue lights. They have special tools such as ____________________ that help them do their jobs.

3. ____________________ travel in special trucks that are usually red. They have special tools such as ____________________ that help them do their jobs.

B. Write the job each person has. Then match each job with its description. Write the letter. (2 marks each)

/8

Job Descriptions

- **A** helps keep dogs and cats healthy and happy
- **B** takes care of people at the hospital
- **C** gives people their yearly physical checkups
- **D** checks and cleans people's teeth

1.

d__________ ◯

2.

d__________ ◯

3.

v__________ ◯

4.

n__________ ◯

Total /20

Test 7

- workers' uniforms and vehicles

Read about what each person on the next page does and fill in the blank. Then decide which uniform and vehicle each person needs and write the letters. (4 marks each)

20

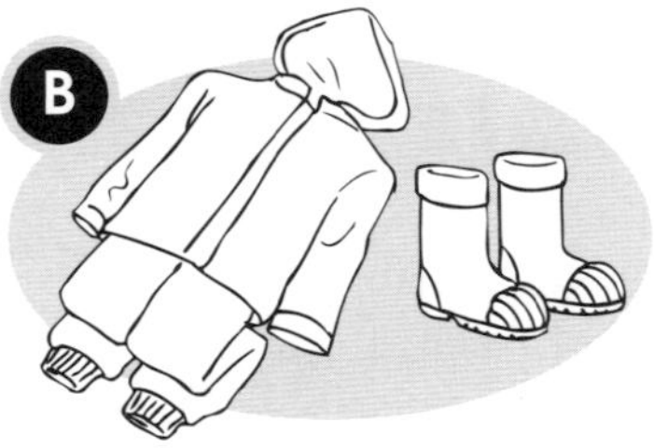

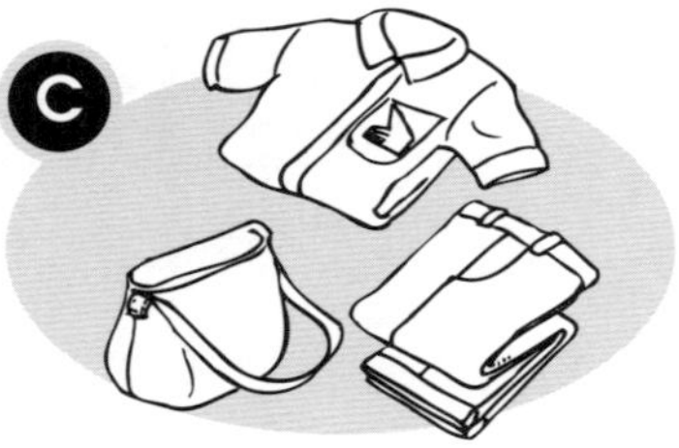

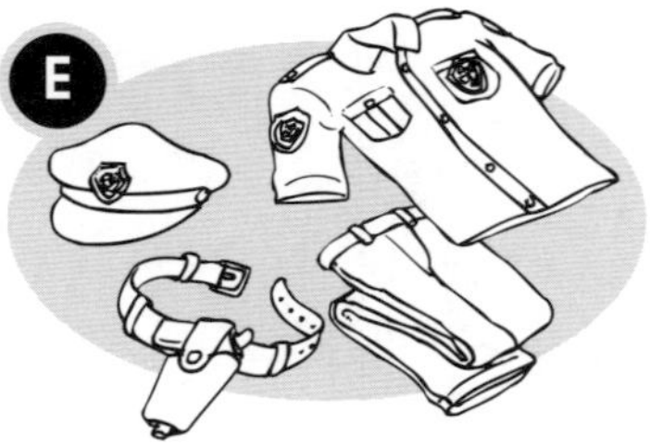

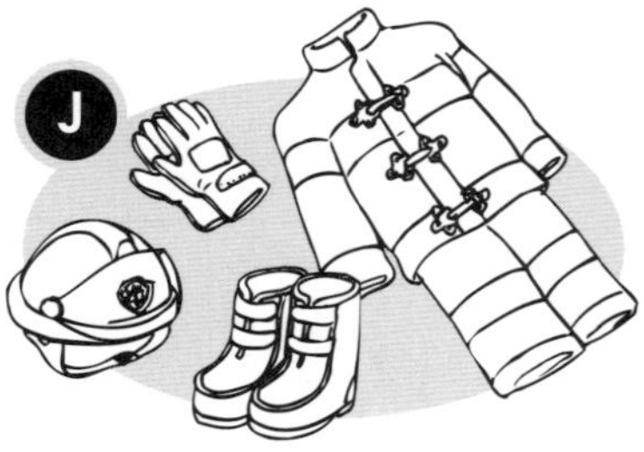

1. 

I sort and deliver mail. I am a ________________ . I need _____ and _____ .

2. 

I catch fish. I am a ________________ .
I need _____ and _____ .

3. She puts out fires. She is a ________________ . She needs _____ and _____ .

4. He gets people to the hospital quickly. He is an ________________ . He needs _____ and _____ .

5. She makes arrests. She is a ________________ . She needs _____ and _____ .

Total
20

BONUS

Guess the job of the person speaking.

"I wear just about anything, as long as it can get dirty. I need canvases, brushes, and paint, but no special vehicle."

____

Bonus
/ 2

Test 8

- maps
- directions

Social Studies

A. Look at the map. Then answer the questions.

(2 marks each)

8

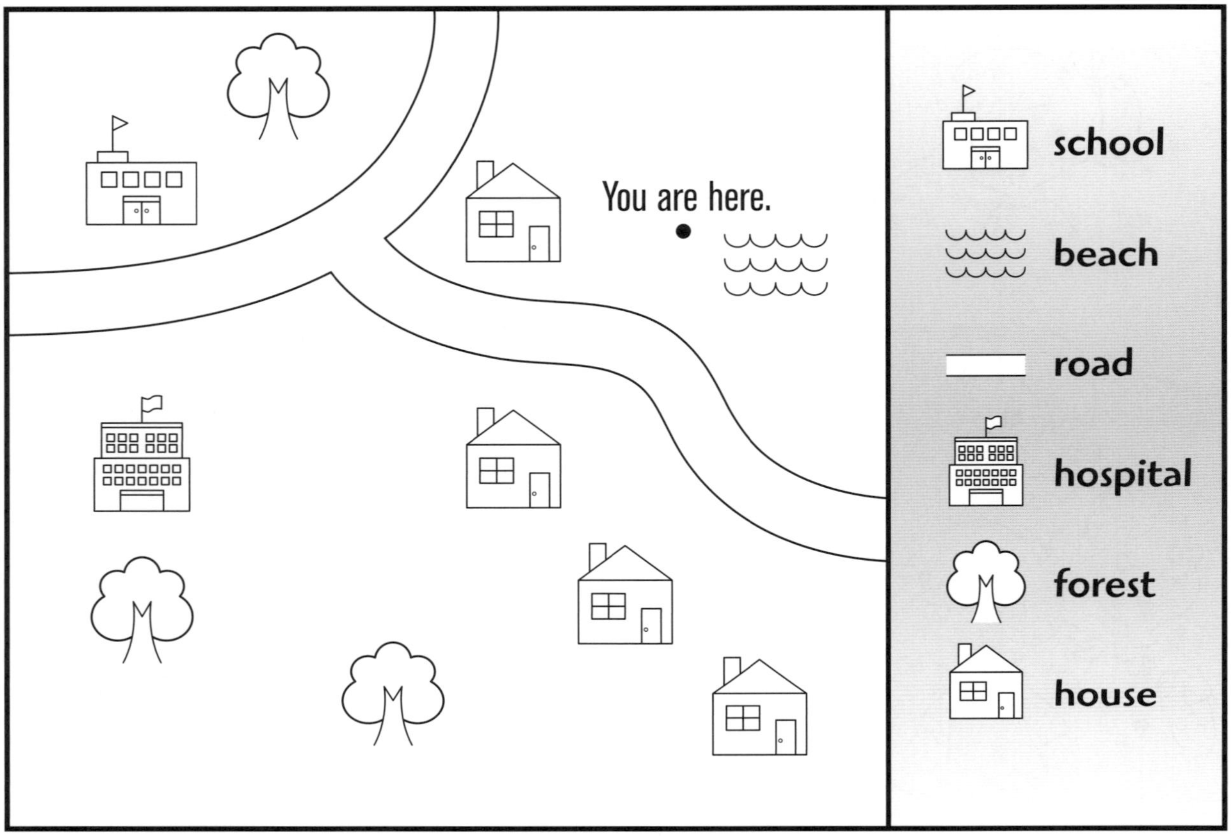

1. What are you closest to? __________

2. Are you closest to a house, a school, or a hospital? __________

3. How many houses are there? __________

4. How many forests are there? __________

B. Use the words "left", "right", "above", "below", or the name of the object to fill in the blanks. (2 marks each)

12

1. The girl is ___________ the driver.

2. The ___________ is left of the guitar.

3. The suitcases are ___________ the balloon.

4. The ladder is ___________ of the balloon.

5. The suitcases are right of the ___________ .

6. All of the objects and people are ___________ of the ladder.

Total

20

Test 9

- **grids**

A. Look at the grid. Write "true" or "false" for each statement. (2 marks each)

8

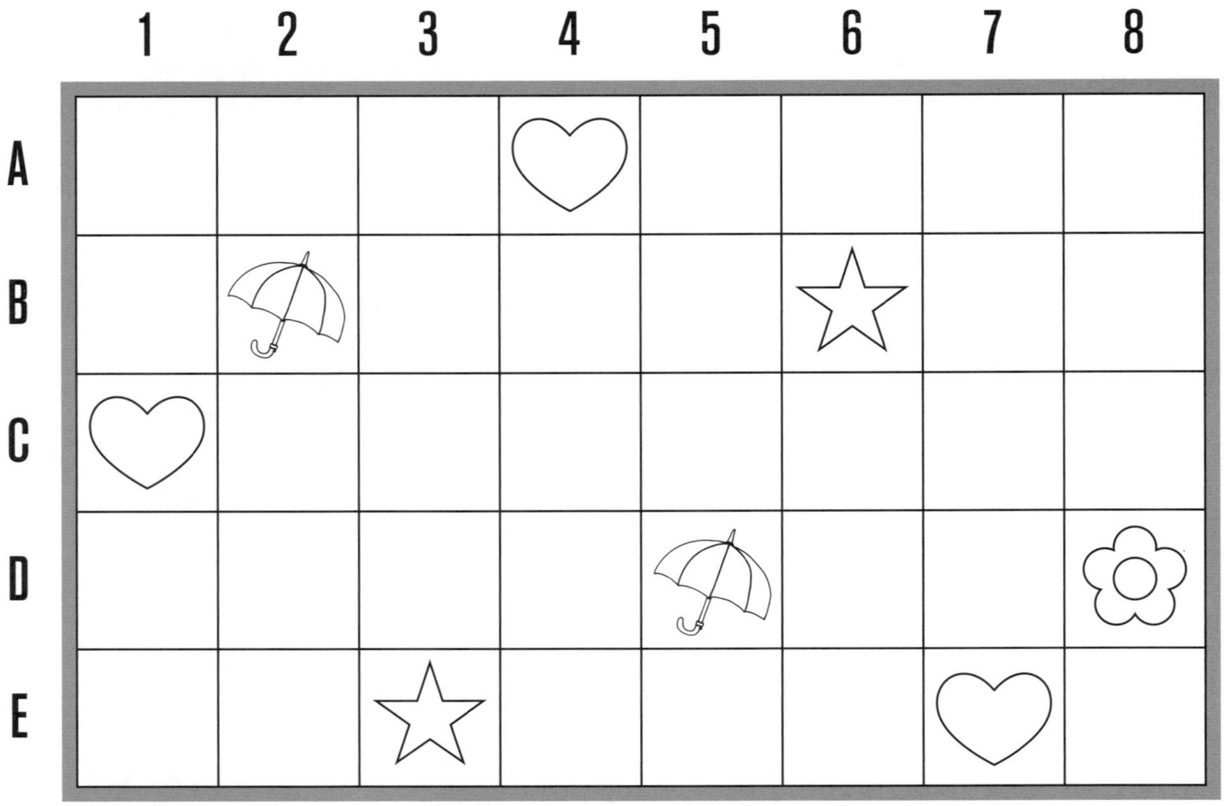

1. The flower is in E8. __________

2. The stars are in E2 and B7. __________

3. The hearts are in C1, A4, and E7. __________

4. The umbrellas are in C2 and D5. __________

Date:

B. Answer the questions. Then complete the grid.
(2 marks each)

12

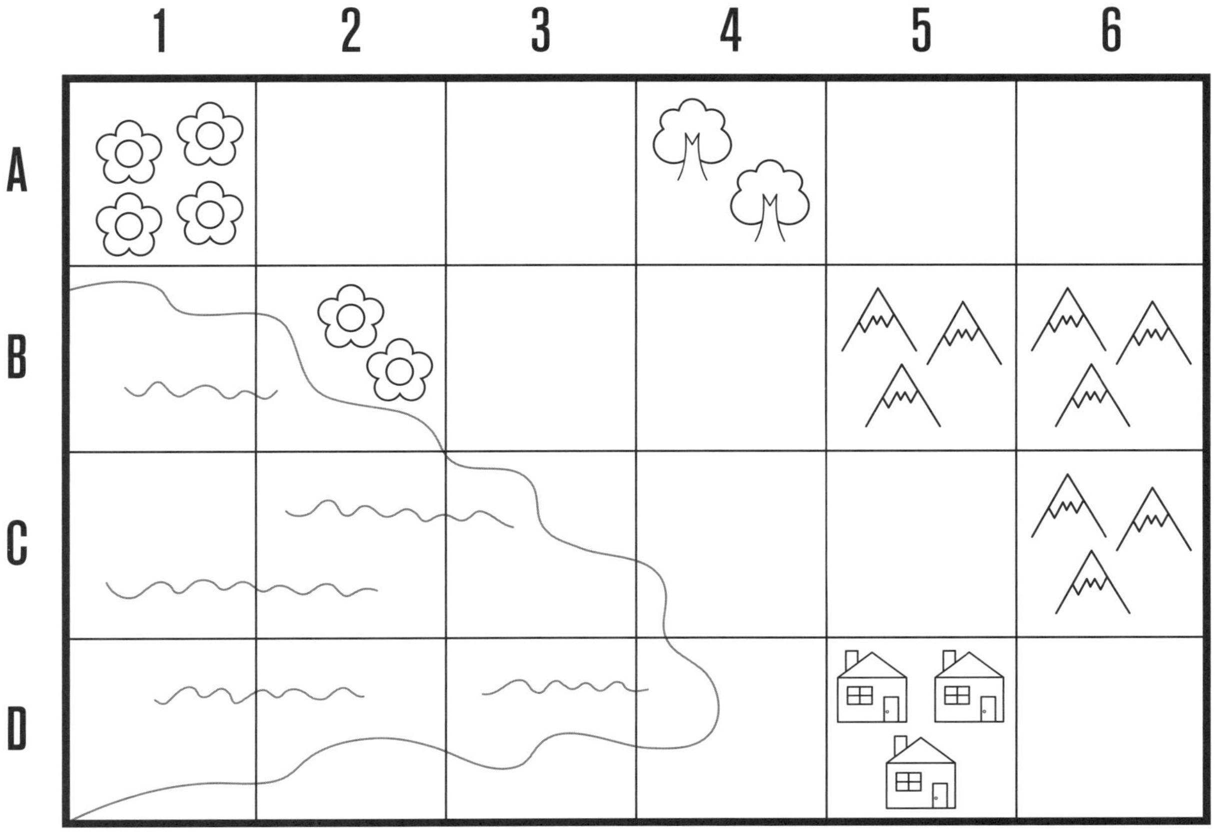

1. Where are the houses? ____________

2. Where are the flowers? ____________

3. Where are the mountains? ____________

4. Where are the trees? ____________

5. Draw a  in C2.

6. Draw a  in A5.

Total

20

Test 10

- **distances and streets on a map**

A. How far is it from one point to another? Use the paddles to find out. (2 marks each)

12

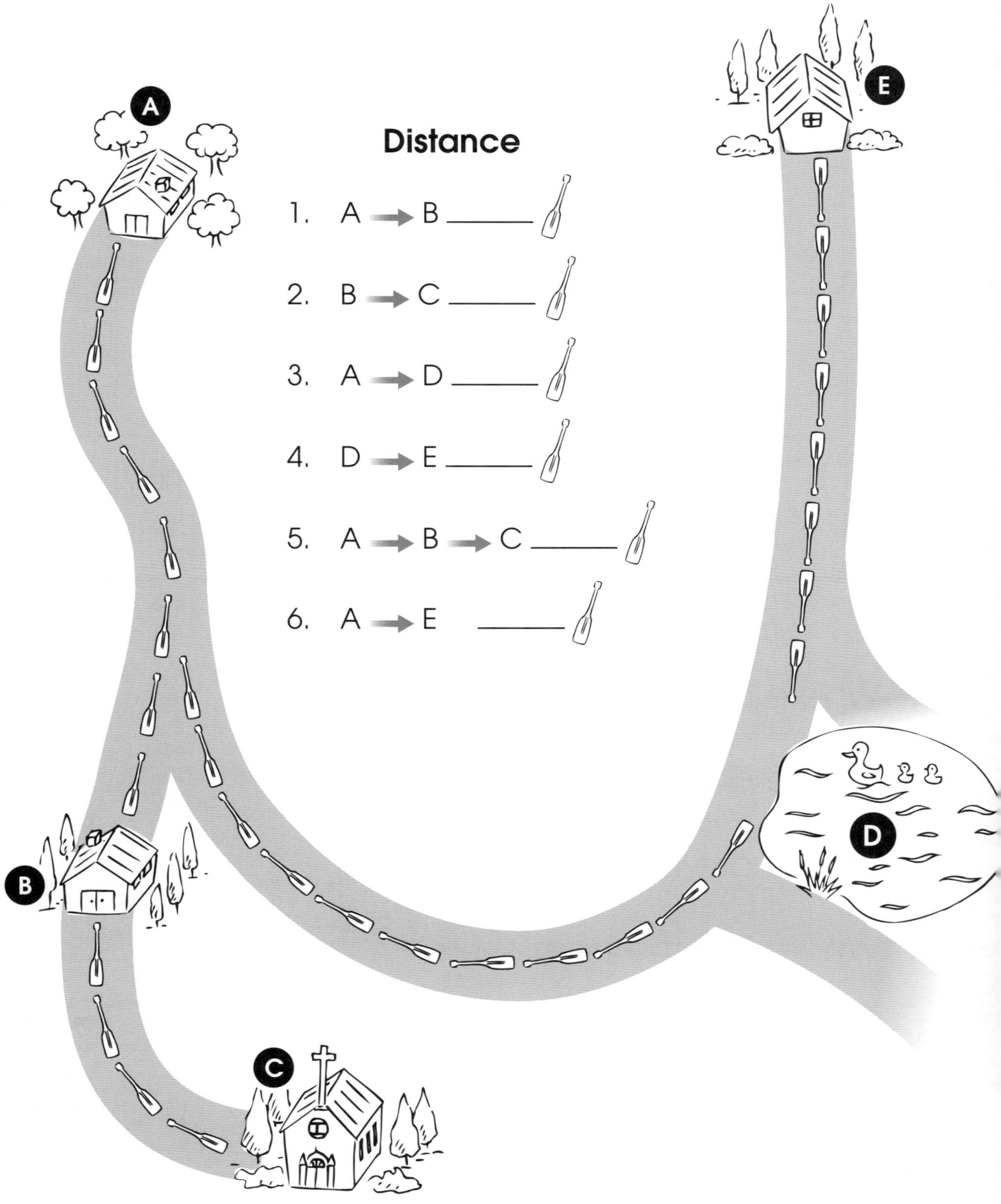

Distance

1. A → B ______
2. B → C ______
3. A → D ______
4. D → E ______
5. A → B → C ______
6. A → E ______

B. Look at the map. Then answer the questions.
(2 marks each)

8

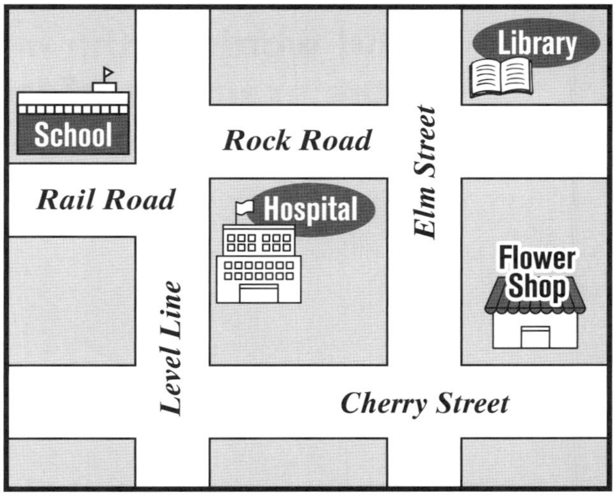

1. On which street is the flower shop?

   ____

2. The library is at the corner of Elm Street and which other street?

   ____

3. Which building is at the corner of Rail Road and Level Line?

   ____

4. Which building is at the corner of Rock Road and Level Line?

   ____

Total
20

BONUS

Draw a square on the map to show the location of the bakery.

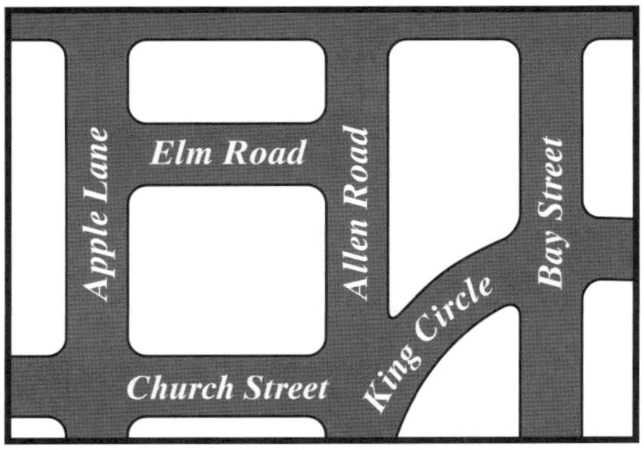

The bakery is at the corner of Allen Road and Church Street.

Bonus
/ 2

Test 11

- landforms and waterways

A. Write the water words in the lake and the land words in the mountain. Then give two more examples of land and water in Canada and write them in the boxes. (1 mark each)

11

island	**plain**	**river**
valley	**waterfall**	**stream**
ocean	**canyon**	**tundra**

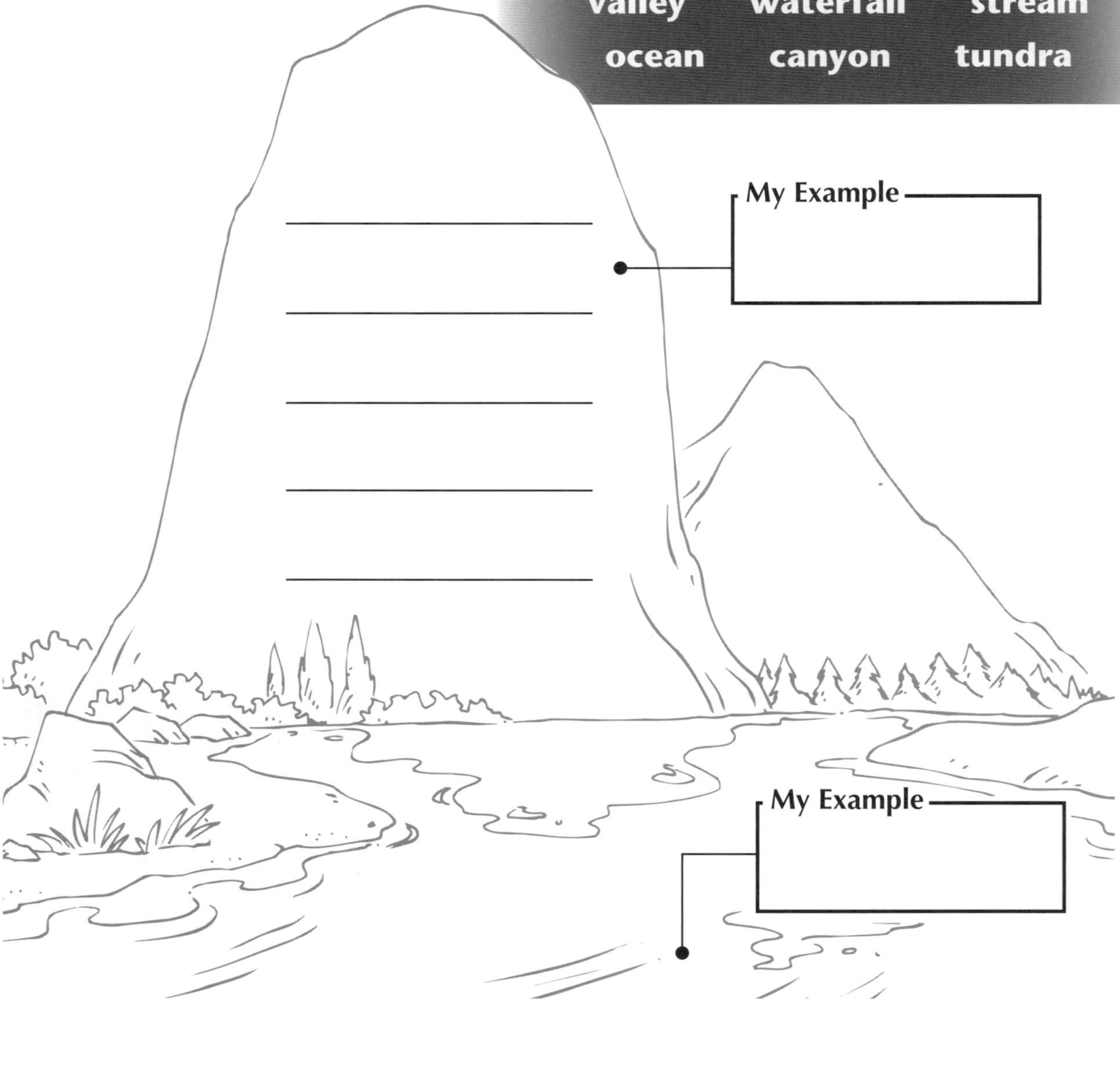

Date:

B. Write which landform or waterway each sentence describes. (3 marks each)

9

1. "I am very steep and much taller than everything around me. My highest point is often a peak." ____________

2. "I am fresh water, not salt water, and I am fed by a river. I don't move much, and I am larger and deeper than a pond." ____________

3. "I flow towards an ocean or a lake, and sometimes I start from a glacier." ____________

Total

20

BONUS

Answer the beaver's question.

Where would you find my house: in a waterway or a landform?

____

Bonus

/2

Test 12

- **Canadian animals**

A. Write the name of the animal being described on the line. (2 marks each)

16

kangaroo **blue whale** **snowy owl** **fox** **lynx** **Canada goose** **elephant** **Arctic hare** **moose** **panda** **porcupine** **black bear**

1. I am a medium-sized wildcat with a black stripe of fur on each ear.

   ____

2. I am quite small, but I have sharp quills all over my body to protect myself.

   ____

3. I am almost all white, and I usually live where it is very cold. I am the official bird of Quebec.

   ____

4. I am the second largest land animal in Canada, and I defend myself with my huge antlers.

   ____

5. I eat plants and animals. I am usually black, but sometimes I am also reddish or brown.

   ____

6. I am the largest animal in the world. I live in the ocean, but I breathe air, just like a human.

____

7. I have a black head and a thick, white ring around my neck. I fly south in fall and north in spring.

____

8. My fur is red, and I have a white belly. I eat mostly animals, but sometimes I eat apples and berries.

____

B. Match the Canadian coin with the name of the animal whose picture is on it. (1 mark each)

4

- beaver
- caribou
- polar bear
- loon

Total

20

Test 13

- **natural and human-built environments**

A. Name the environment in each picture. Then check whether it is natural or human-built. (4 marks each)

16

1.

Ⓐ natural
Ⓑ human-built

2.

Ⓐ natural
Ⓑ human-built

3.

Ⓐ natural
Ⓑ human-built

4.

Ⓐ natural
Ⓑ human-built

B. Look at the map. Then answer the questions.
(2 marks each)

4

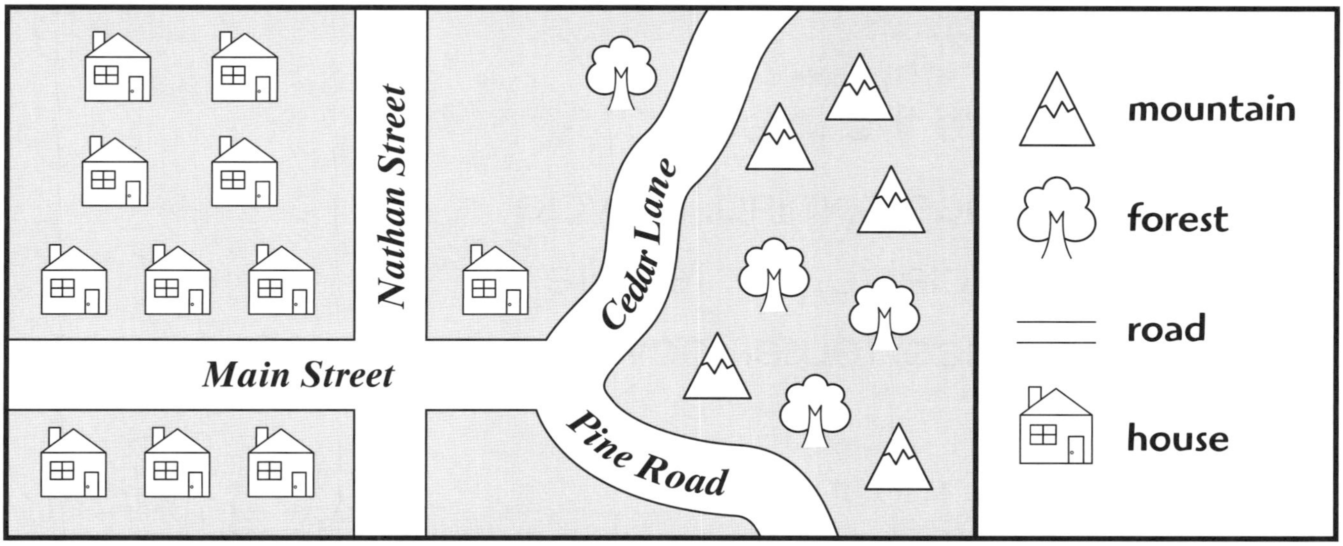

Near which two streets would you find a

1. natural environment?

____

2. human-built environment?

____

Total
20

BONUS

Look at the map above. Then answer the question.

As the human-built environment gets bigger, what do you think will happen to the natural environment?

____

Bonus
/ 2

Test 14

- **the three Rs**

A. Check the correct answers. (2 marks each)

8

1. What are the three Rs?
   - (A) reduce, remind, recycle
   - (B) recycle, rewire, require
   - (C) reduce, reuse, recycle

2. Reduce means to:
   - (A) make more garbage.
   - (B) make less noise in class.
   - (C) make less garbage.

3. Reuse means to:
   - (A) use something once and throw it away.
   - (B) use something more than once.
   - (C) use five things at once.

4. Recycle means to:
   - (A) make something new from something old.
   - (B) put something in the garbage.
   - (C) burn garbage.

B. Decide whether the children are reducing, reusing, or recycling. Write it on the line. (2 marks each)

12

1. Barbara gets a lot of her clothing from her older sister. ____________

2. Aaron does not buy bottles of water. He uses his own container instead. ____________

3. Mike collects pop can tabs. They are melted down and used to make wheelchairs. ____________

4. Lee puts his birthday gift wrap in the blue bin. ____________

5. Anna does not print out web pages. She reads them off the screen. ____________

6. 

____

Total

20

Social Studies

Test 15

- tools

A. Match the tool with the description of a job it is needed for. Write the letter in the circle.
(2 marks each)

14

- **A** cleaning up spilt cereal
- **B** listening to your favourite band
- **C** baking a cake
- **D** knowing if it is warm enough to play outside
- **E** boiling water for hot chocolate
- **F** reading an email from Grandma
- **G** planting flowers outside

1.
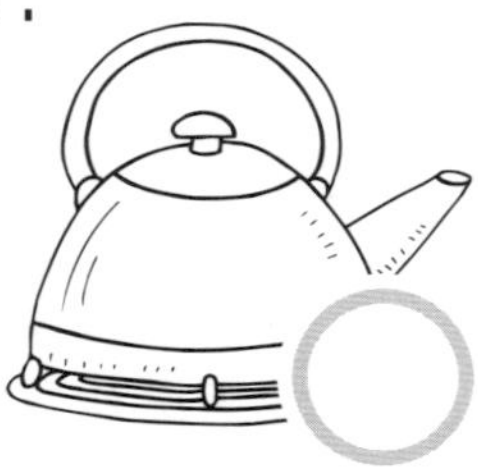

2.
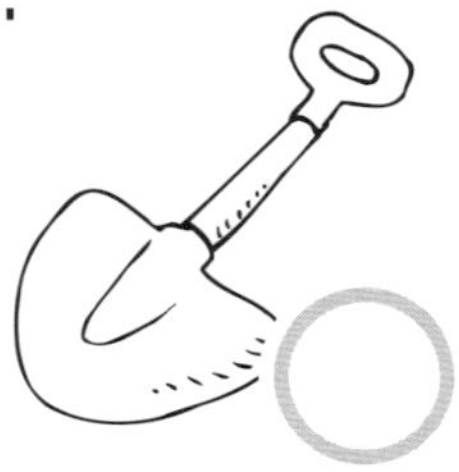

3.
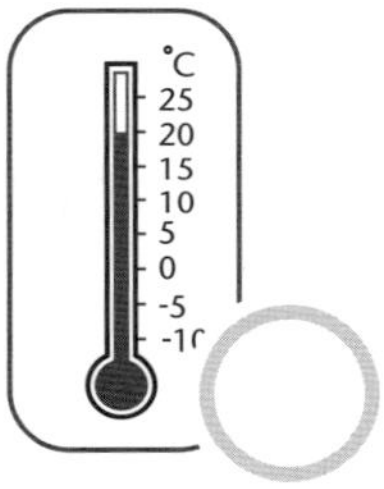

4.
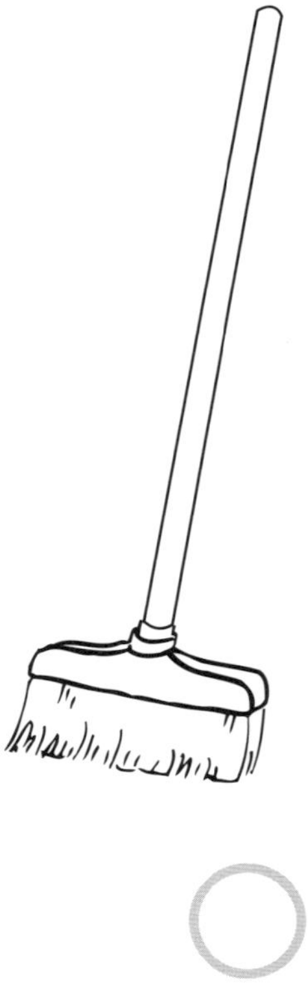

5.

6.

7.

B. Match the new tools with the older versions of them. (2 marks each)

6

 • • 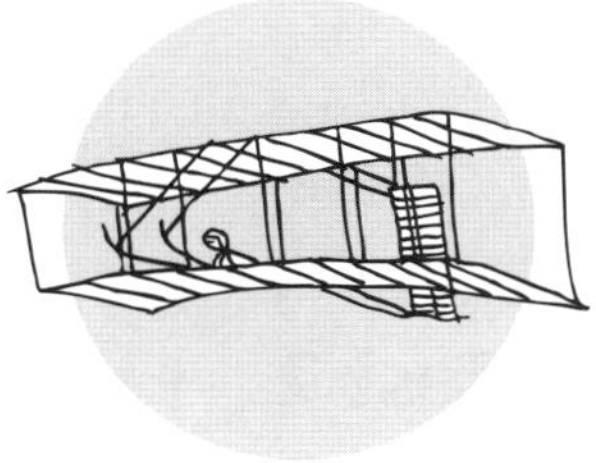

 • • 

 • • 

Total

20

Draw the tool these workers have in common.

- construction worker
- house painter
- firefighter

Bonus

/2

My Test Record

Test 1

- responsibilities
- rules

____ / 20

Test 2

- rules, responsibilities, and relationships

____ / 20

Test 3

- types of community
- community needs

____ / 20

Test 4

- travelling in a community
- community signs

____ / 20

Test 5

- different jobs in a community

____ / 20

Test 6

- safety workers
- health workers

____ / 20

Test 7

- workers' uniforms and vehicles

____ / 20

Test 8

- maps
- directions

____ / 20

Test 9

- grids

____ / 20

Test 10

- distances and streets on a map

____ / 20

Test 11

- landforms and waterways

____ / 20

Test 12

- Canadian animals

____ / 20

Test 13

- natural and human-built environments

____ / 20

Test 14

- the three Rs

____ / 20

Test 15

- tools

____ / 20

TestSmart

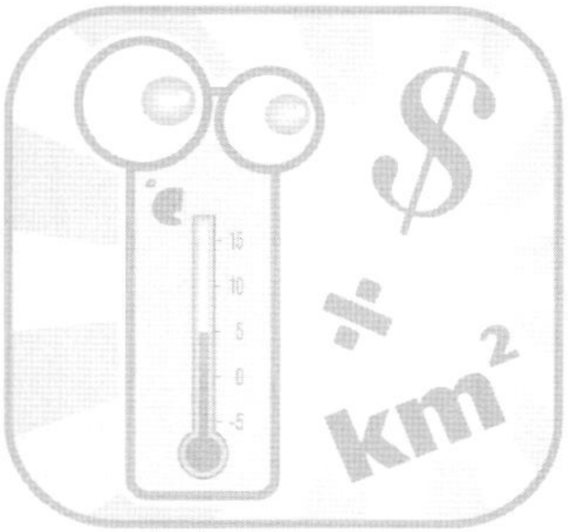

Science

Science

Test 1

- our bodies

A. Name the parts of the body. Then write what each body part does. (1 mark each)

10

What the Body Part Does

breathe see move touch taste

function: ____________

function: ____________

function: ____________

function: ____________

function: ____________

B. Look at each animal. Write how it moves and what body part it uses to move. (2 marks each)

4

1.

how it moves: ____________________

body parts used: ____________________

2.

how it moves: ____________________

body parts used: ____________________

C. What parts of the body do the jobs below? Fill in the blanks. (2 marks each)

6

1. Joanne bites an apple with her ________________ .

2. Grandma threads a needle with her ________________ .

3. Mr. Smith lifts the heavy boxes with his strong ________________ .

Total

20

Test 2

- our senses

A. Write the missing letters of our five senses. Then write what sense you would use to know about each group of things. (1 mark each)

10

Five Senses

1. sm ___ ___ ___ 2. to ___ ___ ___

3. t ___ ___ t ___ 4. s ___ e 5. h ___ ___ r

6. ________________

7. ________________

8. ________________

9. ________________

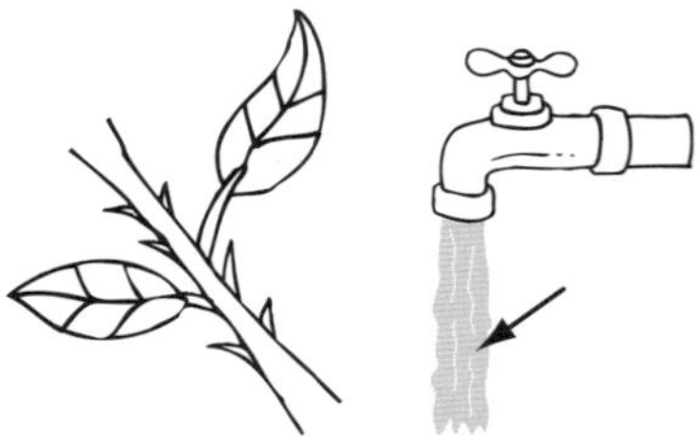

10. ________________

Date:

B. Circle two senses that you can use to find out about each thing. (2 marks each)

4

1. **someone laughing**

see taste smell hear

2. **ice cream**

smell touch hear taste

C. Write the thing that can be used to protect our sense in each situation. (2 marks each)

6

1.

____

2.

____

3.

____

Total

20

Test 3

- living things and their growth

A. Check the picture if it shows a living thing.

(1 mark each)

4

A

B

C

D

E

F

B. Give an example of a living thing in each category. (2 marks each)

4

plant: ________________ animal: ________________

Date:

C. Put the pictures in order to show the growth of the living things. Write 1, 2, and 3. (2 marks each)

4

1.

2.

D. Draw lines to show what these young living things become when they mature. (2 marks each)

8

1. a seed •
2. a caterpillar •
3. an egg •
4. a puppy •

Total

20

Test 4

Science

- characteristics of living things

A. Find out what living things need with the help of the pictures. (2 marks each)

6

Living things need...

B. See what the living things do to get the things they need. Fill in the blanks. (2 marks each)

6

1. Cacti can store a lot of ____________ .

2. Plants make ____________ in their leaves.

3. Whales breathe ____________ through a blowhole.

C. Complete the pattern on each animal. Then give an example of an animal that has the same pattern. (4 marks each)

8

1.

example

2.

example

BONUS

Total

20

Name the pattern you see on the tree trunk.

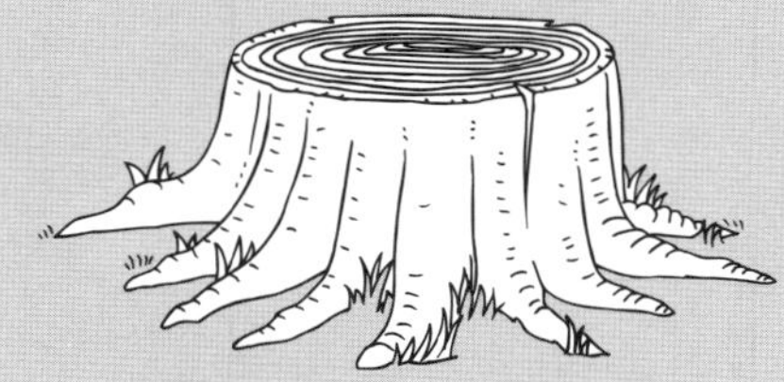

Bonus

/ 2

Test 5

- **healthy eating**

A. Draw lines to match the food items with the correct groups. (1 mark each)

8

Grain Products •

Fruits and Vegetables •

Milk Products •

Meat and Alternatives •

Date:

B. Give an example of a food item that belongs to each group, but is different from the ones on the previous page. (2 marks each)

8

Grain Products: ____________________

Fruits and Vegetables: ____________________

Milk Products: ____________________

Meat and Alternatives: ____________________

C. Put a cross on the food item in each group that is not a healthy choice. (1 mark each)

4

1.

2.

3.

4.

Total

20

Test 6

- staying healthy

A. For each pair of pictures, circle the better exercise for your body. (2 marks each)

8

1.

2.

3.

4.

B. How do you exercise your body to keep it working well? (3 marks)

3

____

____

C. Check the sentences that describe ways we can stay healthy. (1 mark each)

3

Things to Do to Stay Healthy

(A) We exercise regularly.

(B) We get plenty of sleep.

(C) We keep our bodies clean.

(D) We play computer games whenever we want.

(E) We do not wash our hands before having a meal.

D. Circle the child who shows healthy and safe habits in each picture. (2 marks each)

6

1.

2.

3.

Total

20

Test 7

- objects and materials

Science

A. Draw lines to match each object with the material it is made from. Then give another example of an object that is made from that material. (1 mark each)

10

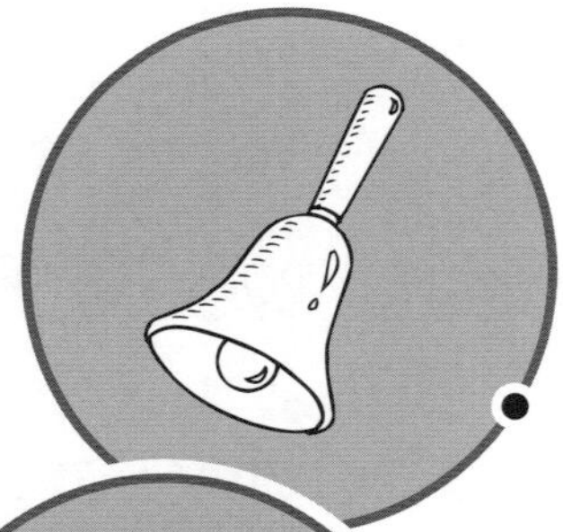

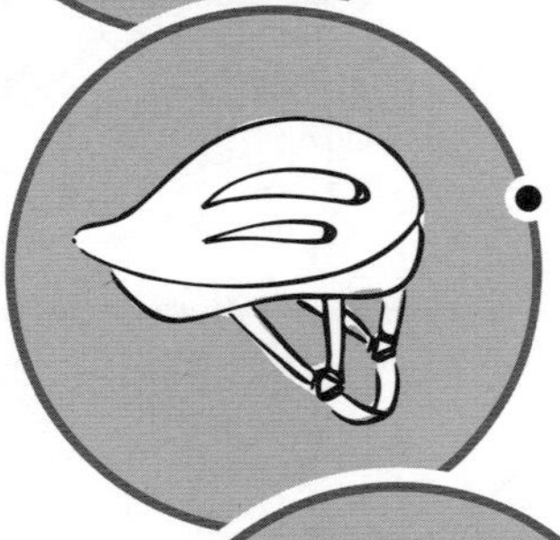

My Example

- cloth: ________________
- wood: ________________
- glass: ________________
- plastic: ________________
- metal: ________________

B. Which materials could be used to make each object? Check the correct answers. (2 marks each)

6

1. **vase**
   - (A) feathers
   - (B) clay
   - (C) glass
   - (D) cloth

2. **paper clip**
   - (A) plastic
   - (B) clay
   - (C) metal
   - (D) grass

3. **food tray**
   - (A) metal
   - (B) sand
   - (C) feathers
   - (D) plastic

C. Which two different materials are used to make the objects? Write the answers on the lines. (2 marks each)

4

1.

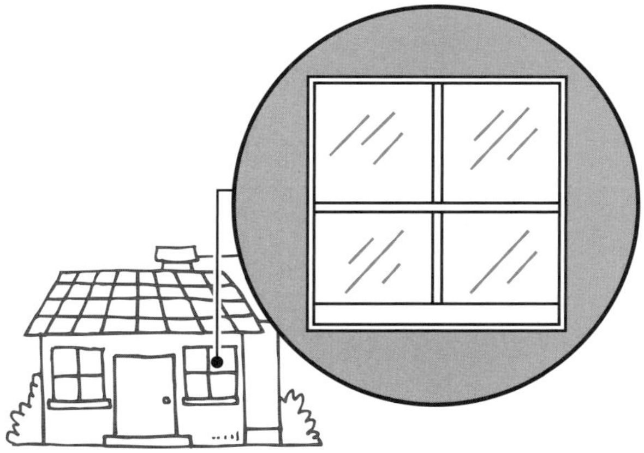

____

____

2.

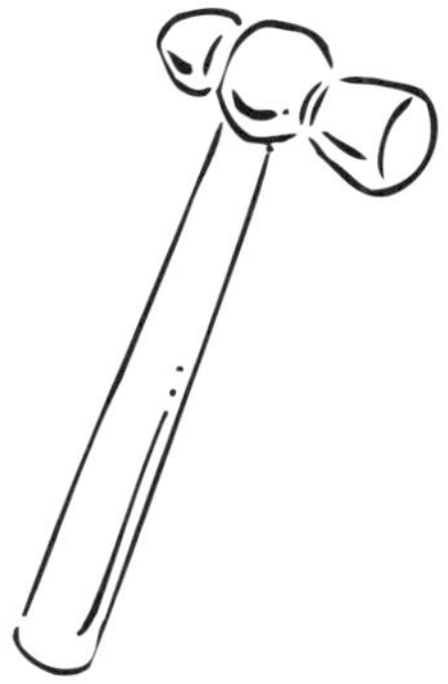

____

____

Total

20

Test 8

- **sources and properties of materials**

A. Write the material that each object is made from. Then circle the word that describes the source of the material. (2 marks each)

8

1\.

material: ____________________

source: animals / plants / the Earth

2\.

material: ____________________

source: animals / plants / the Earth

3\.

material: ____________________

source: animals / plants / the Earth

4\.

material: ____________________

source: animals / plants / the Earth

Date:

B. Circle the words that describe the material each object is made from. (2 marks each)

4

1.

hard soft

light heavy

2.

shiny

dull

floats when placed in water

sinks when placed in water

C. Suggest a material that could be used to make the object. Then describe the material. (2 marks each)

8

Object	Material	Description
Pillow	feathers	
Paperweight		heavy
Tire		

Total

20

BONUS

A metal hat can give your head full protection. Do you think a hat made from metal is a good choice? Explain.

____

____

Bonus

/2

Test 9

- more about properties of materials

A. Draw lines to match the materials that need to be joined with the materials that will join them. (2 marks each)

8

1.

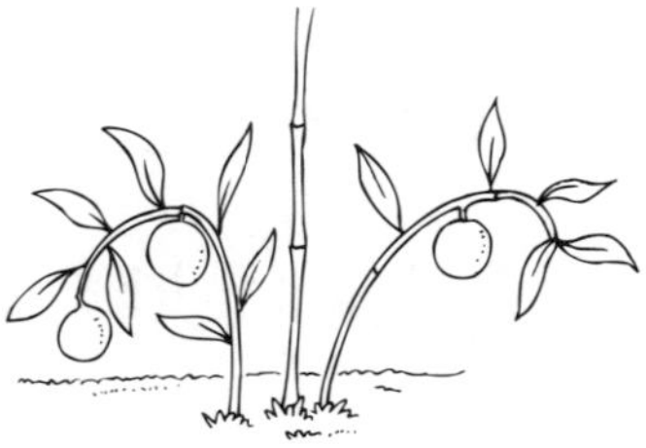

2.

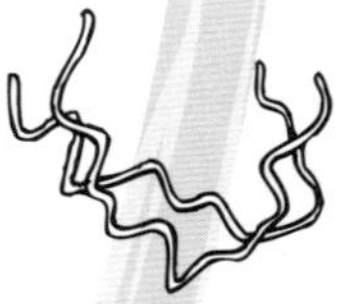

3.

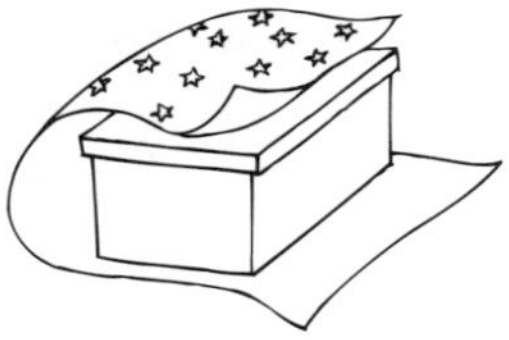

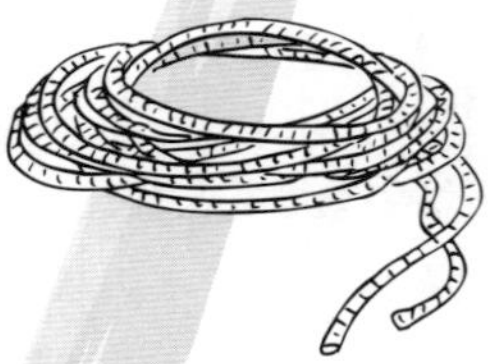

4.

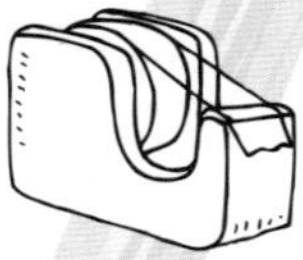

Date:

B. Draw a material that can be used to join the front parts of a jacket. (3 marks)

3

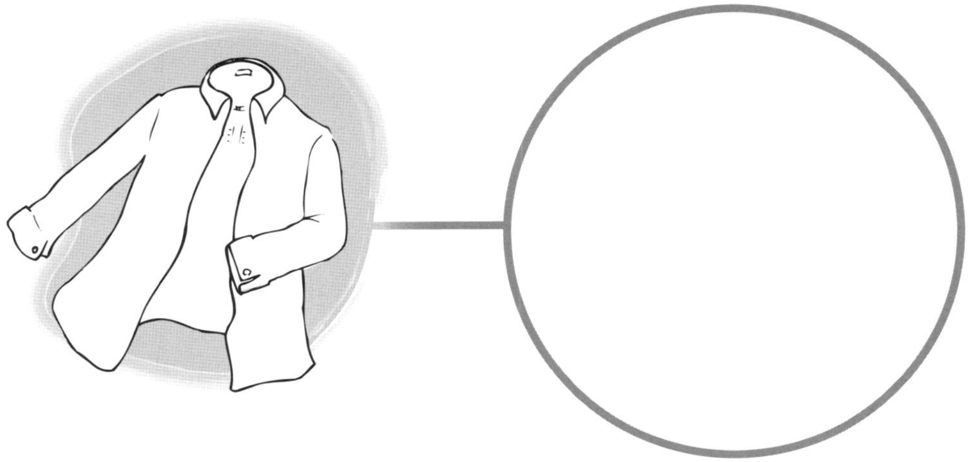

C. Put the pictures in order from 1 to 3 to show the change in the materials. Then circle the correct answer. (3 marks each)

9

1.

2.

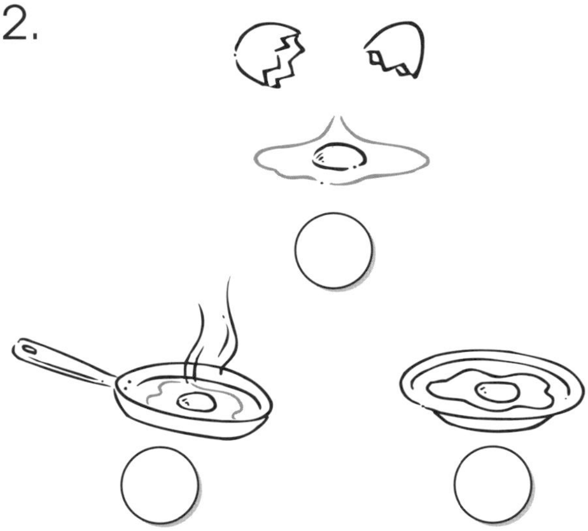

3. The materials above changed due to a change in

colour / temperature / shape .

Total

20

Test 10

- **energy and the sun**

A. Check the correct answers. (2 marks each)

10

1. What produces most of the energy found on Earth?

Ⓐ 

Ⓑ 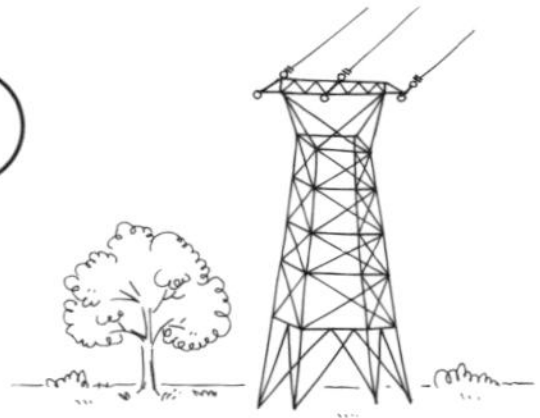

Ⓒ 

2. What gets energy from the sun to live and grow?

Ⓐ animals Ⓑ cars Ⓒ plants

3. What do we get when we eat food?

Ⓐ water Ⓑ energy Ⓒ air

4. What do we need to work properly?

Ⓐ money Ⓑ assignments Ⓒ energy

5. Without the sun,

Ⓐ there would be no life on Earth.

Ⓑ only animals would be found on Earth.

Ⓒ only plants would be found on Earth.

B. Fill in the missing letters to complete the names of the energy givers. Then draw lines to match the energy users with their energy givers. (2 marks each)

10

Energy Givers

e _ _ _ t _ i _ _ ty •

g _ s •

m _ _ cl _ s •

w _ _ d •

s _ _ •

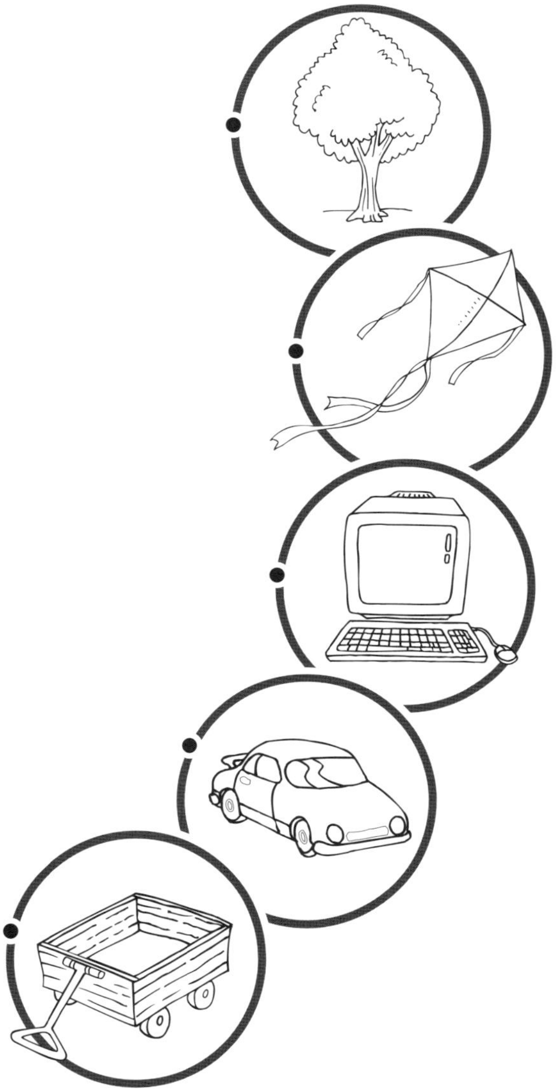

Total

20

BONUS

Name the kind of energy this energy giver provides.

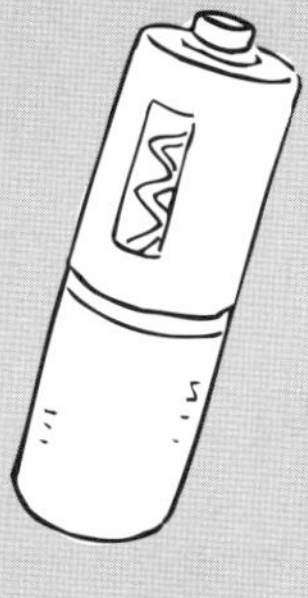

____

Bonus

/ 2

Test 11

- electricity and smart energy use

A. Check the object if it uses electricity as its energy source; otherwise, put a cross. (1 mark each)

8

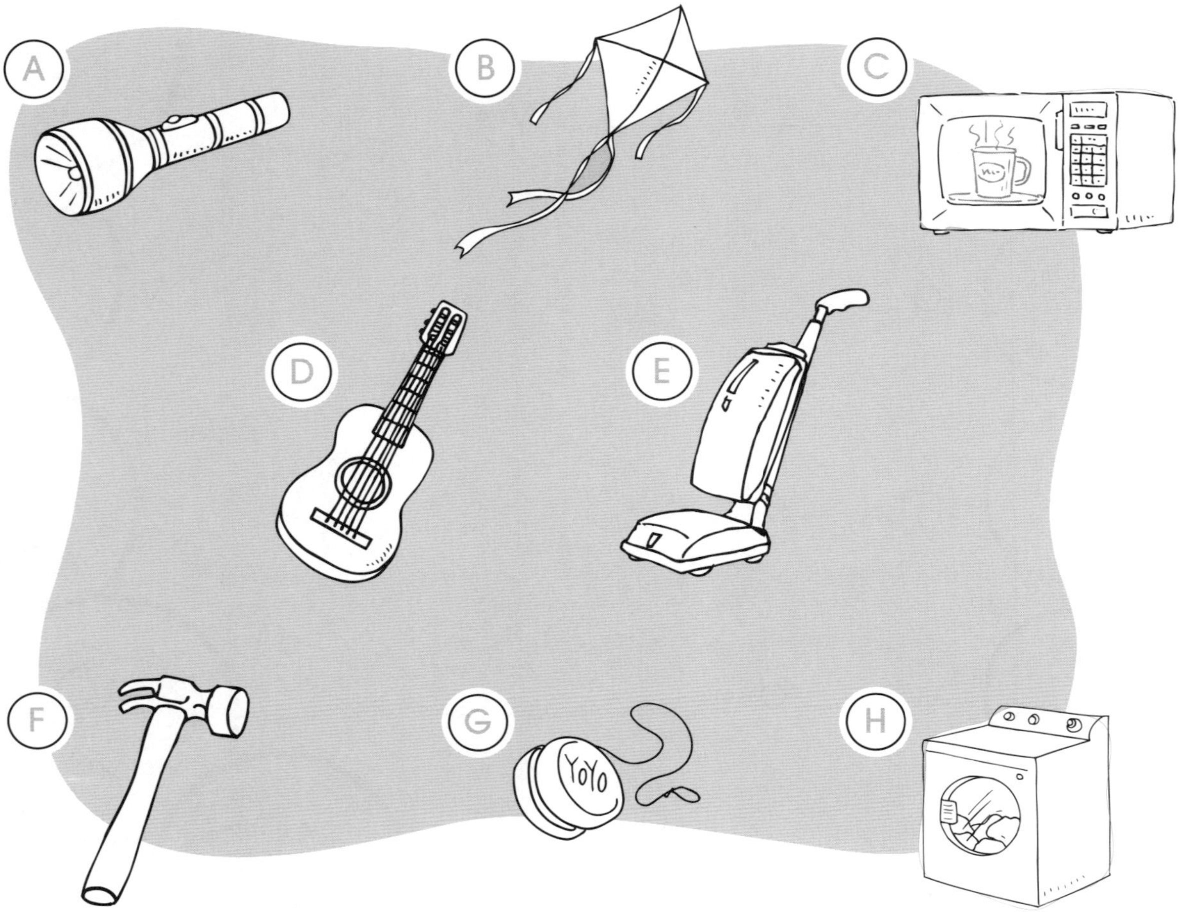

B. Give an example of an object at each place that uses electricity as its energy source. (2 marks each)

4

at home: ____________________

at school: ____________________

C. Check the picture that shows the smarter use of energy. (2 marks each)

4

1. **Ways to Dry Clothes**

2. **No One at Home**

D. What is the smarter way to use energy in each situation? Check the correct letter. (2 marks each)

4

1. When you want to read a bedtime story,

   (A) turn all the bedroom lights on.

   (B) turn your bedside lamp on.

2. When just your jeans are dirty, you may

   (A) wait to wash them until the laundry basket is full.

   (B) wash them in the washing machine right away.

Total 20

Test 12

- food chains and energy

A. Check the correct food chains and put a cross for the wrong ones. (1 mark each)

4

A

B

C

D

B. Draw three arrows to complete the food chain.

(2 marks each)

6

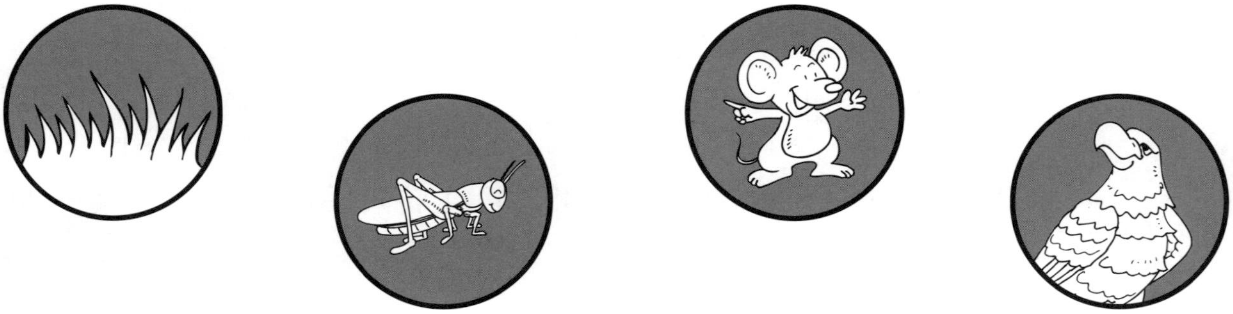

C. Circle the correct pictures to complete the food chain. (3 marks each)

6

1.

2.

D. Put the activities in order from the one that takes the least amount of energy to the one that takes the most. (1 mark each)

4

(A) walking

(B) playing basketball

(C) reading books

(D) sleeping

Energy Used

Total

20

Test 13

- day and night

A. Decide whether you would do each activity during the day or during the night. Draw a ☀ or ☾ in the box. (2 marks each)

8

1.

2.

3.

4.

B. Write two things that you do every day.
(2 marks each)

4

Things I do every day

- ______________________________
- ______________________________

C. Fill in the blanks with "day" or "night". Then colour the parts of the Earth as indicated. (1 mark each)

4

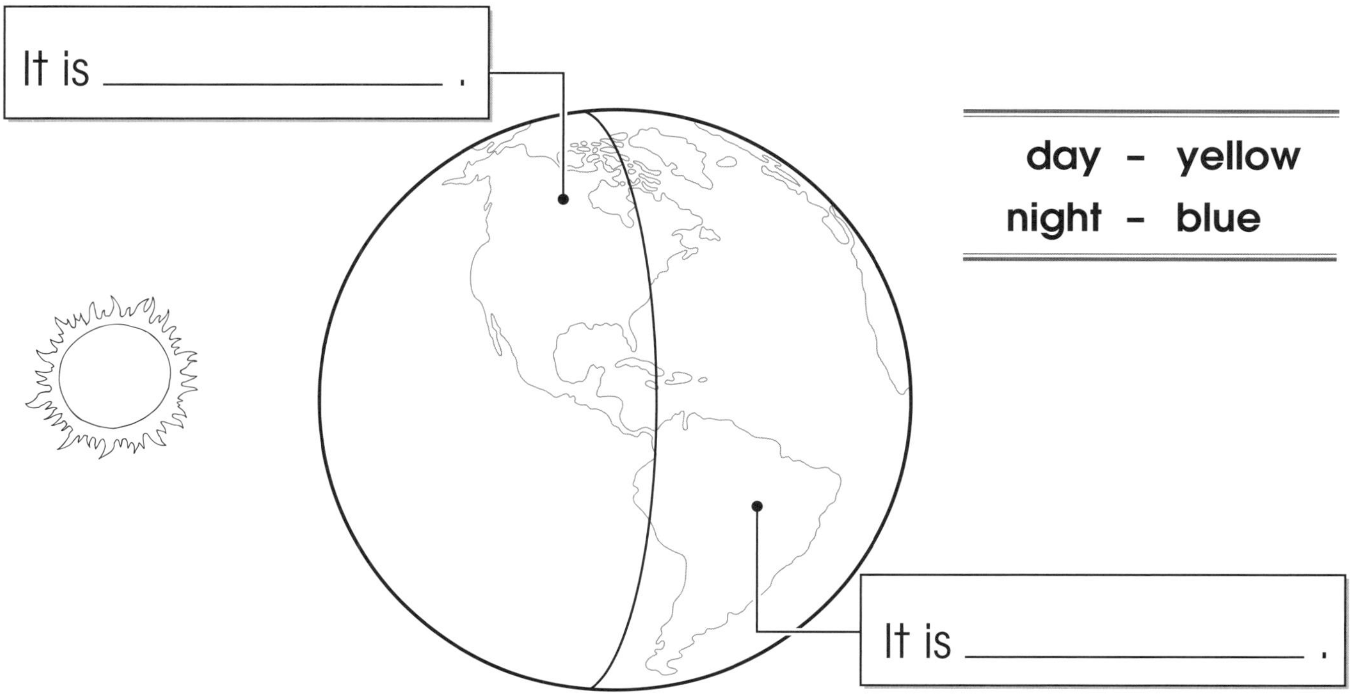

day - yellow
night - blue

D. Match the shadows with the correct times of the day. Write the letters. (2 marks each)

4

A

B

morning: ◯

evening: ◯

Total

20

Test 14

- seasons

A. Write the names of the four seasons in the boxes. Then match the objects with the correct seasons. (2 marks each)

8

Date:

B. Name the season for each of these changes.
(2 marks each)

12

1. Snow falls.

____

2. Trees are green and flowers are in bloom.

____

3. Birds that have been away for the winter return.

____

4. Daylight is long; nights are shorter.

____

5. Some leaves turn yellow, brown, or red.

____

6. Bears wake up after a long sleep.

____

Total

20

BONUS

Name a tree that stays green all year long.

____

Bonus

/ 2

Test 15

- **human activities and plants in different seasons**

A. Name an outdoor activity that you can do in each season. (2 marks each)

8

Activity

spring: ______________________

summer: ______________________

fall: ______________________

winter: ______________________

B. Is the work related to summer or winter? Write the seasons on the lines. (1 mark each)

4

A ______________________

B ______________________

C ______________________

D ______________________

Date:

C. Write the correct season for each picture. Then draw arrows to show the life cycle of the tree.
(1 mark each)

8

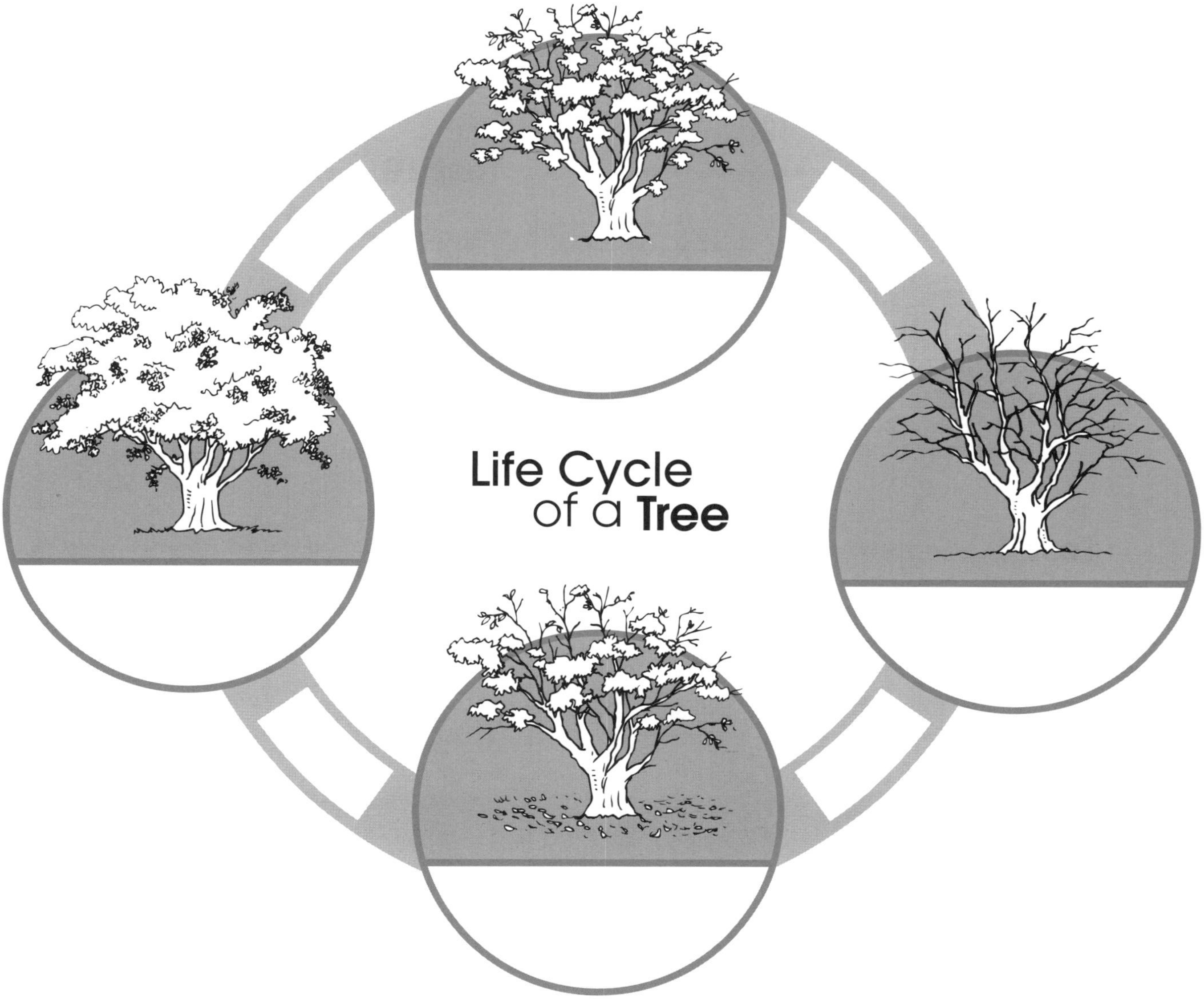

Total
20

Write a food item that you would have in each season.

summer: ____________________

winter: ____________________

Bonus
/ 2

Science

My Test Record

Test 1
- our bodies

___ / 20

Test 2
- our senses

___ / 20

Test 3
- living things and their growth

___ / 20

Test 4
- characteristics of living things

___ / 20

Test 5
- healthy eating

___ / 20

Test 6
- staying healthy

___ / 20

Test 7
- objects and materials

___ / 20

Test 8
- sources and properties of materials

___ / 20

Test 9
- more about properties of materials

___ / 20

Test 10
- energy and the sun

___ / 20

Test 11
- electricity and smart energy use

___ / 20

Test 12
- food chains and energy

___ / 20

Test 13
- day and night

___ / 20

Test 14
- seasons

___ / 20

Test 15
- human activities and plants in different seasons

___ / 20

English

Test 1

A. A: ✔ B: ✔
C: ✘ D: ✘
E: ✔

B. 1. A 2. C
3. B 4. B
5. A

Test 2

A. 1. B 2. C

B. 1. x 2. c
3. n 4. p
5. f 6. s

C. 1. card 2. goat
3. pin 4. bear
5. jar 6. fish

Bonus
1. kick 2. roar
3. tint

Test 3

A. 1. Gregory 2. Marvin
3. Henry 4. Buster
5. Rosa

B. 1. T 2. F
3. T 4. T
5. F 6. T

C. D

Test 4

A. 1. A 2. B

B. 1. i 2. a
3. o 4. e

C. 1. cane 2. prize
3. cone 4. cube
5. sweep 6. cute
7. acorn

Bonus
blew ; moose ; jewel ; view

Test 5

A. A: ✔ B: ✘
C: ✔ D: ✔
E: ✘ F: ✔

B. 1. dream 2. pirates
3. ocean 4. buried
5. parrot 6. flowers
7. treasure

Test 6

A. 1. C 2. A

B. 1. floor 2. fill
3. rare 4. tent
5. wand

C. (Suggested answers)
1. phone 2. trunk
3. coat 4. hen

Bonus
(Suggested answers)
wing ; ring ; thing ; king

Test 7

A. 1. Ping Pong 2. King Kong

B. 1. T 2. T
3. F 4. F
5. T 6. F

C. 1-2. two big, black buttons / a long carrot
3-4. two chocolate cookies / a big potato

Test 8

A. 1. B 2. C

B. 1. cat ; mouse 2. flowers ; garden
3. girl ; picture 4. story ; king

C. 1. Ottawa 2. David
3. WALL-E 4. Barbie

D. 1. elephant 2. library
3. doctor

Test 9

A. 1. crow 2. bee
3. bear 4. dogs
5. frogs

B. 1. It made footprints.
2. A bee is buzzing in the tree.
3. There are two frogs. /
There are a couple of frogs.

Test 10

A. 1. A 2. B
B. 1. ducks 2. house
3. tomatoes
C. 1. sisters 2. boots
3. squirrel 4. sandwiches
5. story 6. parks
Bonus
1. fairies 2. leaves
3. salmon

Test 11

A. A; C
B. Maple
May 15
Chris
June 24
Parkside
Miss Green
Angela
C. 1. last summer 2. in New York

Test 12

A. 1. A 2. C
B. 1. an 2. a
C. 1. an 2. the
3. an 4. the
5. the 6. a
7. A
Bonus
1. a 2. an

Test 13

A. 1. The kitten likes drinking milk.
2. The sun is shining brightly. /
The sun is brightly shining.
3. We play ball games at recess.
4. This book belongs to Kate.
B. (Suggested answers)
1. Sam and James are making a mask.
2. Tim is walking his dog in the rain.

Test 14

A. A: ✔ B: ✘
C: ✔ D: ✘
E: ✔ F: ✘
G: ✔ H: ✘
B. 1. fruit 2. board
3. bananas 4. blender
5. smooth 6. two

Test 15

A. 1. B 2. A
B. 1. the waiter 2. Karen
3. this book 4. the dogs over there
C. 1. they 2. I
3. you 4. we
D. 1. It 2. We
3. You 4. She
5. They

Test 16

A.

B.
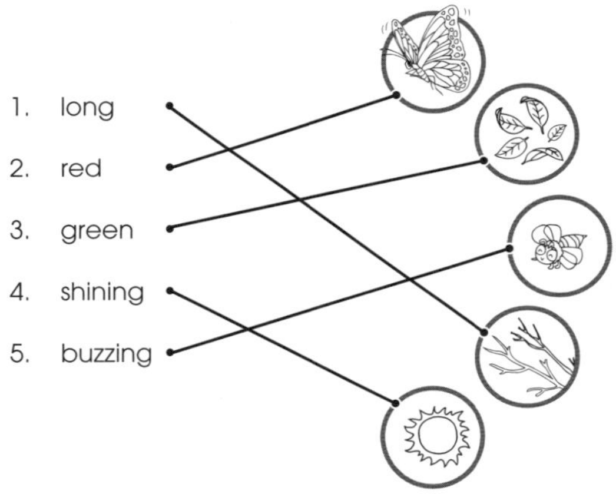

C. 1. He lives in a nest (in a forest).
2. The forest floor is a long way down.

Test 17

A. 1. C 2. B
B. 1. drives 2. Colour
3. buy 4. borrow
5. sleeps 6. collect
C. 1. swing 2. push
3. run 4. slide
5. clap 6. jump
Bonus
(Suggested answer)
All classes meet in the hall before the outing.

Test 18

A. 1. B   2. A
3. C

B. 1. castle   2. happy
3. village   4. blue
5. red   6. king

C. They bought both a red quilt and a blue one.

Test 19

A. 1. A   2. C

B. 1. colour   2. disk
3. height

C. 1. cute ; black ; short
2. big ; long ; sharp

Bonus
huge ; enormous ; giant ; gigantic ; large

Test 20

A. 1.    2. 
3.    4. 
5. 

B. 1. rainbow   2. hears
3. touches   4. rough
5. pizza   6. dessert
7. tastes

C. 1. She touches the big oak tree.
2. It is in the oven.

Test 21

A. 1. A   2. C

B. 1. in   2. on
3. under

C. 1. on   2. under
3. above   4. in
5. behind   6. beside

Bonus
1. at
2. on

Test 22

A. 1. ate ; made
2. park ; school
3. early ; late
4. drinks ; snacks

B. 1. Dan messaged Jen.
2. Sam's dad made his favourite sandwich.
3. It is in the fridge.

Test 23

A. 1. B   2. C

B. 1.    2. 
3.    4. 

C. Telling Sentences: B ; F
Asking Sentences: A ; C ; G
Surprising Sentences: D ; E

Bonus
1. S   2. T
3. A

Test 24

A. A: butter
B: maple syrup
C: pancakes

B. 1. Grandma came to visit.
2. Grandma made pancakes.
3. Grandma gave Rob a pancake.
4. Rob smeared butter on the pancake.
5. Rob poured maple syrup on the pancake.
6. Rob ate the pancake.

C. She promised to teach Rob how to make pancakes.

Test 25

A. 1. C   2. B

B. 1. .   2. !
3. !   4. ?
5. ?   6. .

C. 1. Christmas tree
2. spider web
3. CN Tower

D. 1. Jasmine and I live on the same street.
2. Can I go to Niagara Falls with you, Dad?
3. What an exciting game!

Test 26

A. (Individual writing)

B. (Individual writing)

Math

Test 1

A. 1. 5 2. 3 3. 8
4. 4 5. 3 6. 6
7. 5 8. 5 9. 3
10. 2

B. 1: one 2: two 3: three
4: four 5: five 6: six
7: seven 8: eight 9: nine
10: ten

Test 2

A. 1. 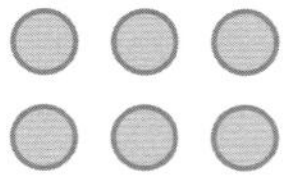 2. 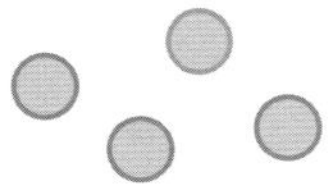

B. 1. A 2. A

C. 1. 5 ; 

2. 3 ; 

3. 4 ; 

D. 1. 4 2. 5

Bonus
Yes

Test 3

A. A ; D

B. 1. 1  2. 3 

3. 2 

C. 1. 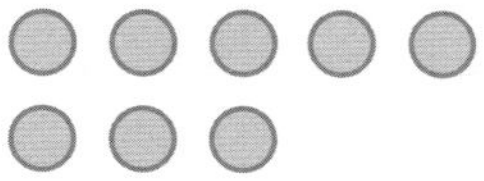 ; 8

2. 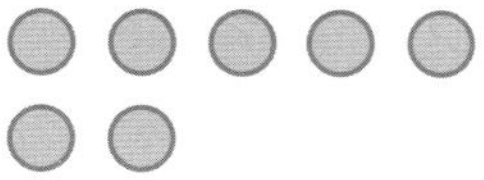 ; 7

3. 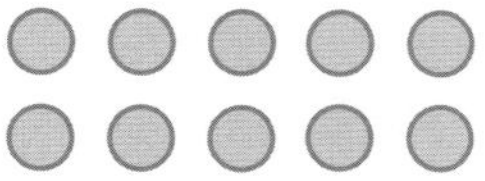 ; 10

4. 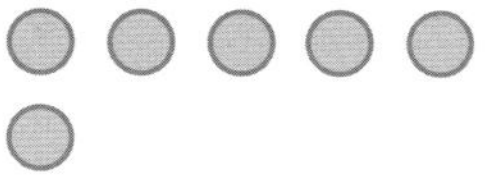 ; 6

Bonus
C

Test 4

A. 1. A 2. B 3. A

B. 1. 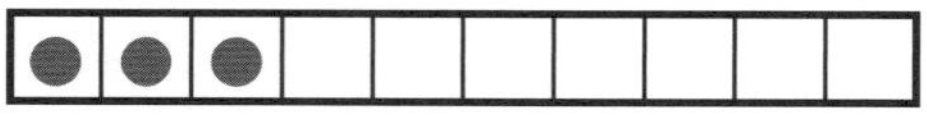 ; 7

2. 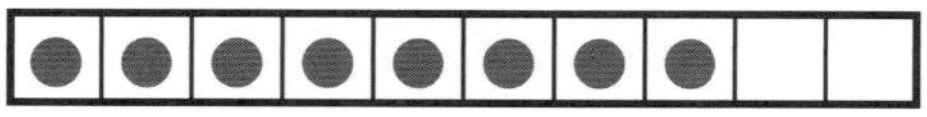 ; 8

C. 1. 8 ; 2
2. 5 is 5 less than 10.
3. 4 is 6 less than 10.
4. 3 is 7 less than 10.
5. 7 is 3 less than 10.

Test 5

A. 1. 7 2. 5 3. 10
B. 1. 7 2. 6 3. 8
C. 1. 7 2. 11 3. 7
4. 5 5. 13 6. 11
7. 8

Bonus
7

Test 6

A. 1. Cross out 1 object. ; 5
2. Cross out 2 objects. ; 5
3. Cross out 4 objects. ; 7
4. Cross out 7 objects. ; 5

B. 1. 6 ; 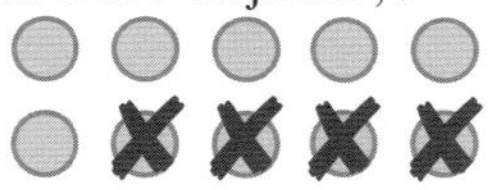

2. 5 ; 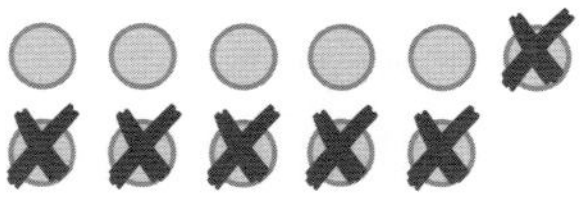

3. 6 ; 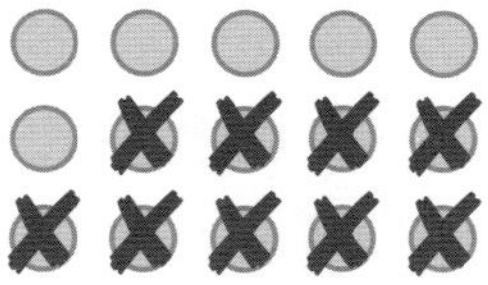

4. 4 ; 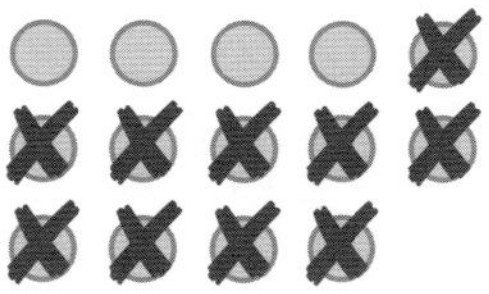

5. 6 ; 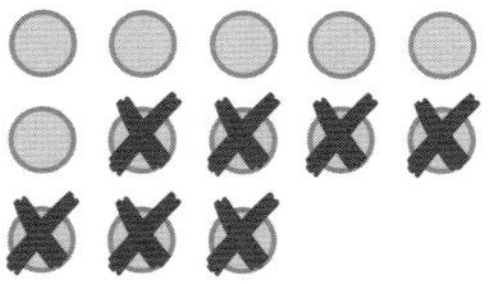

6. 3 ; 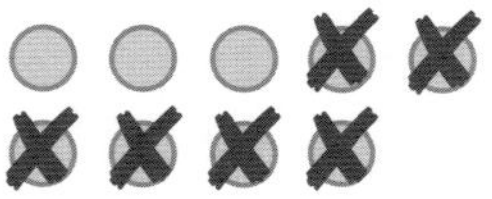

Test 7

A. 1. 5 2. 6 3. 3
4. 3 5. 7 6. 5
7. 5 8. 10

B. 1. 10 2. 5 3. 7
4. 9 5. 12 6. 10

Test 8

A. 1. 7 2. 12

B. 1.
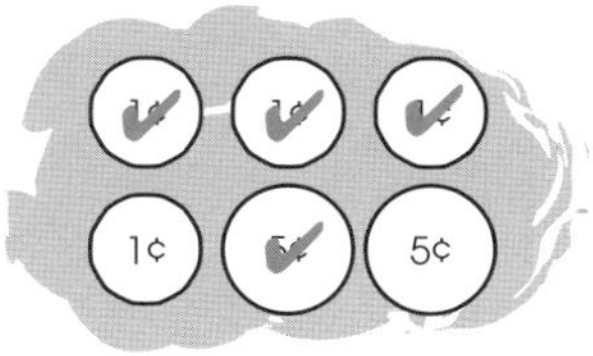
2.
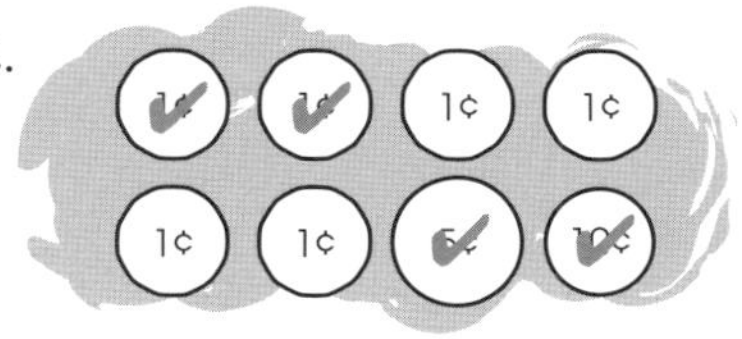

C. 1.
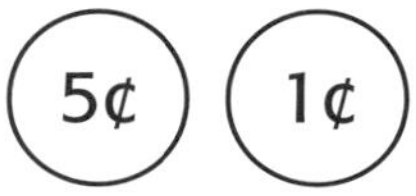

2.
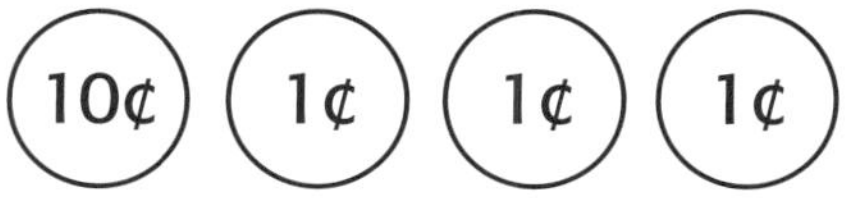

3.

4.
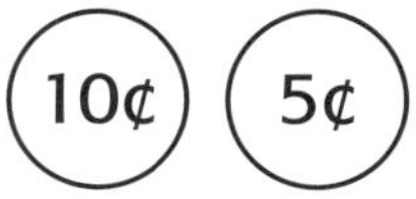

Test 9

A. 1. B 2. A

B. 1. 3 ; afternoon
2. 10 ; night

C. 1.

2.

3.

4.

5.

Test 10

A. Thursday ; Sunday ;
Wednesday ;
Monday ; Saturday ;
Friday ; Tuesday

B. 1. Sunday 2. Tuesday 3. Wednesday

C. Judy's Plan:
Sun: stay with Grandma
Mon: stay with Grandma
Tue: home
Thu: see the dentist
• Wednesday
• Friday and Saturday

Test 11

A. 1. Summer ; 2 2. Winter ; 4
3. Spring ; 1 4. Fall ; 3

B. 1. B ; C 2. A ; B
3. A ; B 4. B ; C

Bonus
Summer

Test 12

A. 1. fourth 2. ninth 3. tenth
4. first

B. 1. second 2. fourth 3. sixth
4. eighth 5. tenth

C.

Bonus
third, fourth

Test 13

A. 1. pencil 2. eraser 3. eraser
4. pen 5. pencil 6. pen

B. 1. shorter 2. taller 3. building
4. tree

Test 14

A. 1-3.

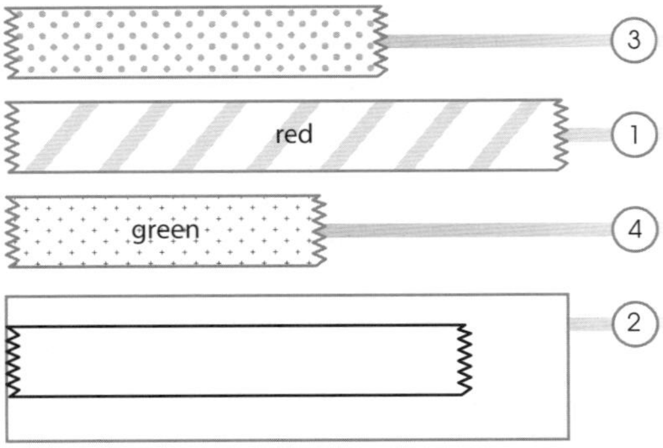

4. 3

B. 1. 9 ; 3 2. 3 ; 3
3. 6 4. the same

Bonus
larger

Test 15

A. 1a. 16 b. 7 c. 10
Circle:

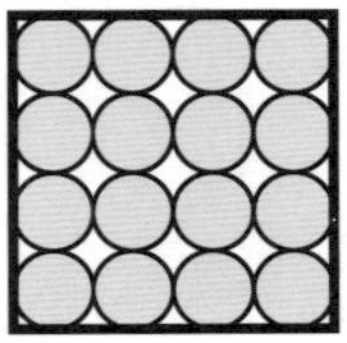

2a. 9 b. 8 c. 12
Circle:

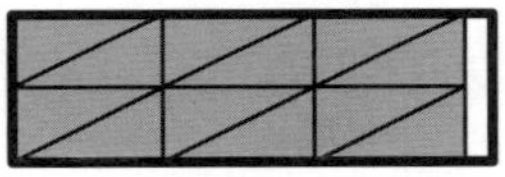

B. 1. 9 ; 8 ; 4 2. A
3. C 4. 4

Test 16

A. 1. bucket 2. milk carton
3. tank 4. bathtub

B. 1. 16 2. 1 3. 40
4. 3 5. 30 6. 5

Test 17

A. 1. shovel 2. pencil
3. ball

B. 1.

2.

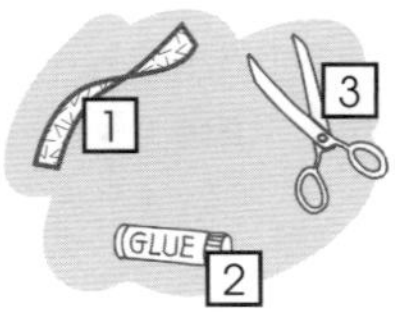

C. 1. A 2. B
3. A 4. B

Test 18

A. 1. Cross out: rectangle
2. Cross out: triangle

B. triangle: B, F
square: D
circle: C, E
rectangle: A

C. 1. 3 2. 4 3. 4
4. 6 5. 4 6. 5

Bonus
C

Test 19

A. 1. rectangular prism ; 4
2. cube ; 2
3. sphere ; 3
4. cylinder ; 5
5. cone ; 1

B. 1.

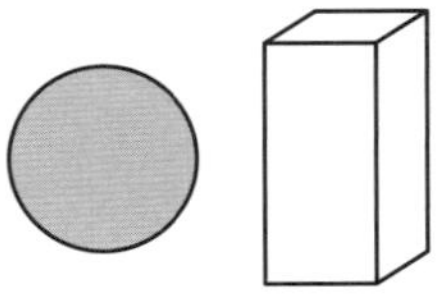

2.

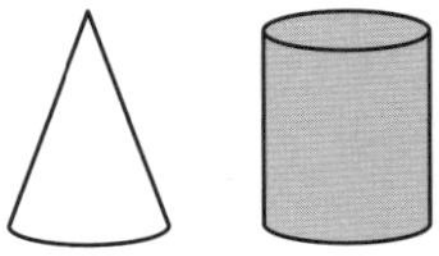

3.

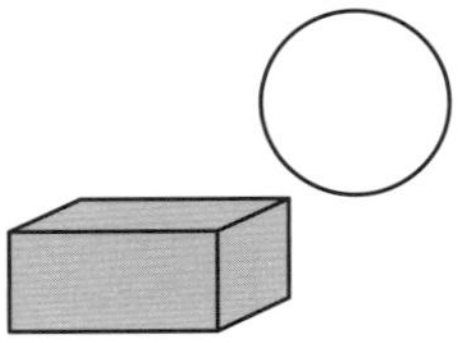

4.

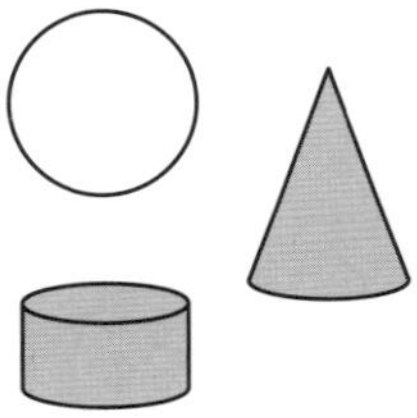

5.

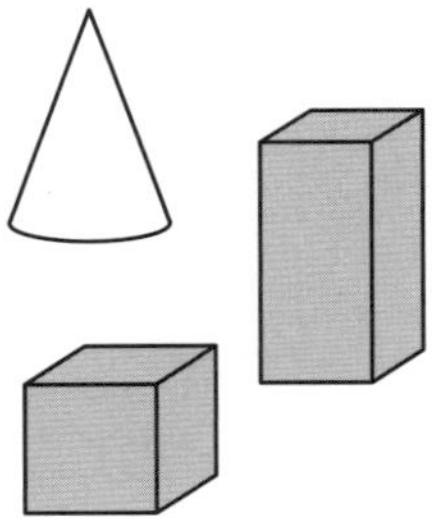

Test 20

A. 1. ✔ 2. ✔
3. ✘ 4. ✘

B.

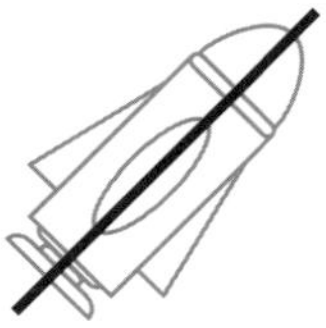

C. 1. 

2. 

3. 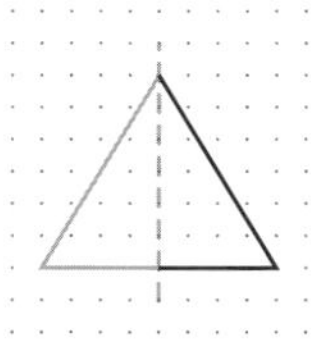

4. 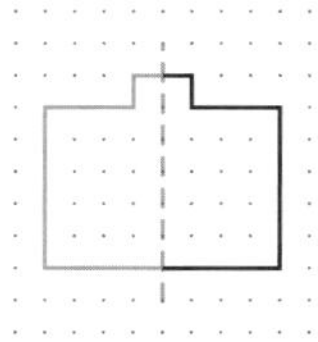

Test 21

A. 1. B 2. A 3. A
4. A

B. 1. in front of 2. in 3. on
4. over 5. behind 6. under

Test 22

A. 1. 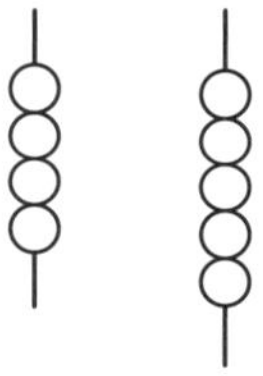

4 ; 5

2. 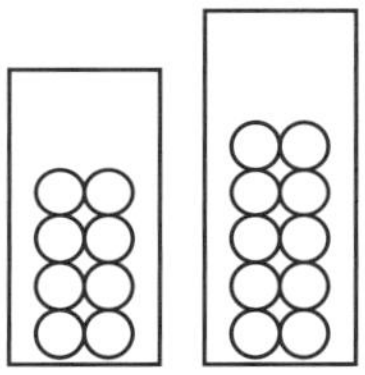

8 ; 10

B. 1. 2's ; 8 ; 10 2. 1's ; 4 ; 5
3. 10's ; 40 ; 50 4. 5's ; 20 ; 25

Bonus
B

Test 23

A. 1. orientation ; 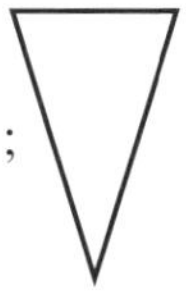 2. size ; 

B. (Individual answer)

C. 1. 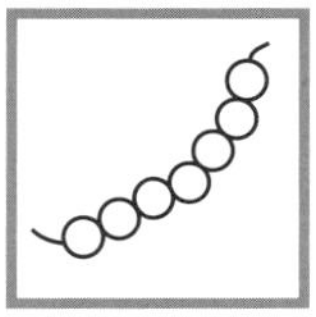

growing

2. 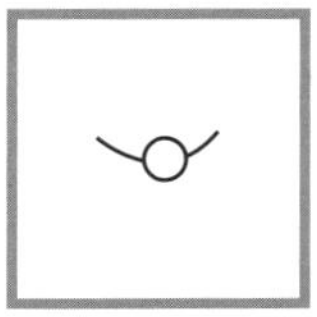

shrinking

Bonus
B

Test 24

A. 1. Cross out: drum stick
2. Cross out: fork

B.

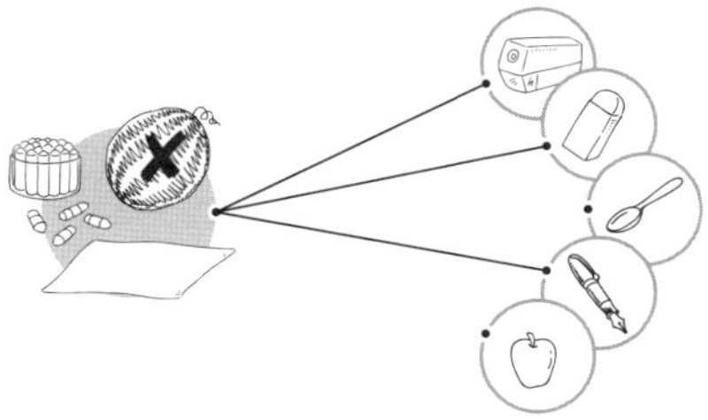

C. (Suggested answers)

1. 

2. 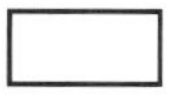

3. 

4. 

Bonus
vegetables ; meat

Test 25

A. 5 ; 4 ; 3 ; 4

B. 1. orange 2. mango
3. 1 more 4. 16 children

C. 1. 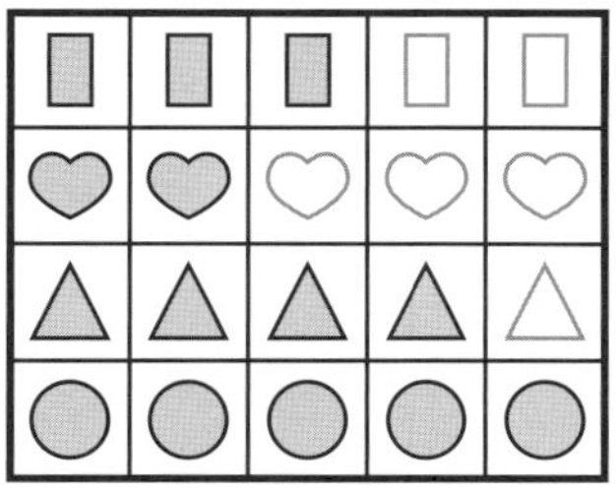

2. 4 3. 2 4. 

Test 26

A.

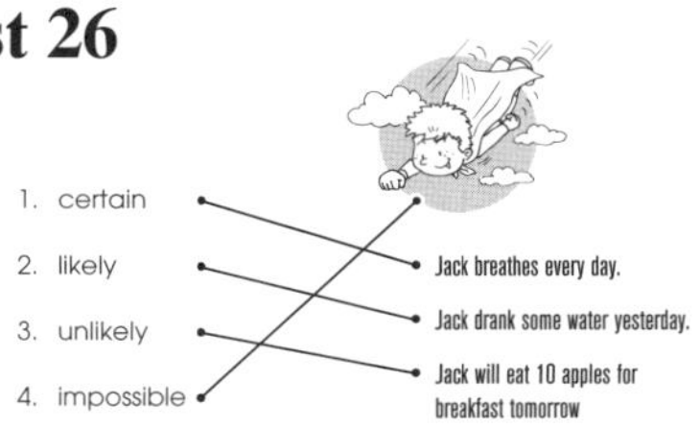

B. 1. A 2. C

C. 1. likely 2. unlikely
3. impossible 4. certain

Bonus

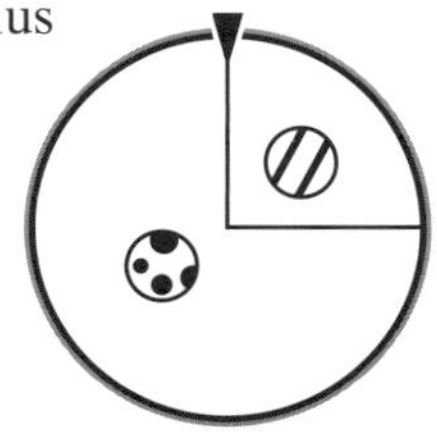

Social Studies

Test 1

A. 1. A ; family
2. B ; child
3. A ; family
4. B ; both

B. 1. B
2. A

Bonus
(Individual answer)

Test 2

A. 1. B ; Responsibilities
2. A ; Rules
3. A ; Responsibilities

B. 1. responsibility
2. rule
3. relationship
4. bigger responsibility

Test 3

A. 1. big city ; skyscrapers, malls, highways
2. rural community ; lakes, rocky, canoe rental shops
3. farm community ; barns, fields, tractor repair shops

B. 1. doctor
2. library
3. post box
4. restaurant

Test 4

A. 1. by bus
2. by bicycle
3. by car
4. walking
5-6. walking / by bicycle

B. 1. rules
2. safe
3.

4.

Test 5

A. 1. zoo keeper ; D ; J
2. teacher ; C ; E
3. farmer ; B ; H
4. baker ; F ; I
5. mail carrier ; A ; G

B. 1. product
2. tool
3. product
4. tool
5. construction worker

Bonus
Apples come from orchards. They are grown by farmers.

Test 6

A. 1. B ; E
2. Police officers ; police dogs
3. Firefighters ; ladders

B. 1. doctor ; C
2. dentist ; D
3. vet ; A
4. nurse ; B

Test 7

1. mail carrier ; C ; I
2. fisherwoman ; B ; F
3. firefighter ; D ; J
4. ambulance driver ; G ; H
5. police officer ; A ; E

Bonus
artist

Test 8

A. 1. beach
2. house
3. four
4. three

B. 1. above
2. driver
3. below
4. right
5. guitar
6. left

Test 9

A. 1. false
   2. false
   3. true
   4. false

B. 1. D5
   2. A1 ; B2
   3. B5 ; B6 ; C6
   4. A4
   5-6.

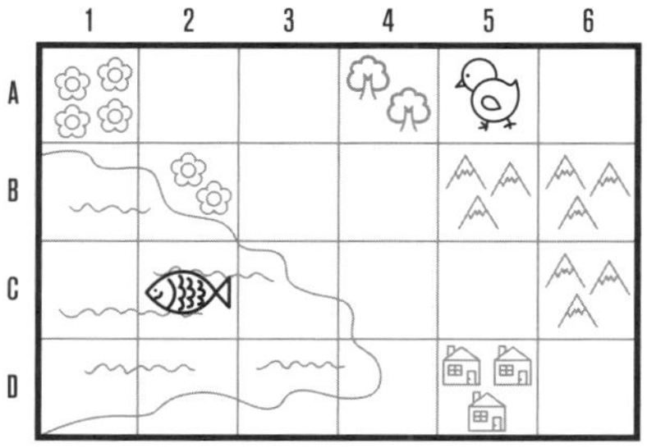

Test 10

A. 1. 8
   2. 4
   3. 17
   4. 8
   5. 12
   6. 25

B. 1. Cherry Street
   2. Rock Road
   3. the school
   4. the hospital

Bonus

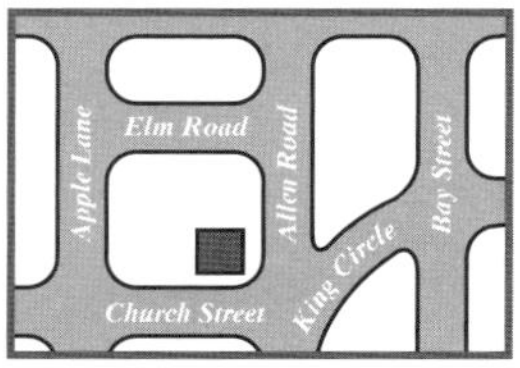

Test 11

A. (Individual examples)
   in the mountain: island ; plain ; valley ; canyon ; tundra
   in the lake: river ; waterfall ; stream ; ocean

B. 1. mountain 2. lake 3. river

Bonus
   in a waterway

Test 12

A. 1. lynx 2. porcupine
   3. snowy owl 4. moose
   5. black bear 6. blue whale
   7. Canada goose 8. fox

B.

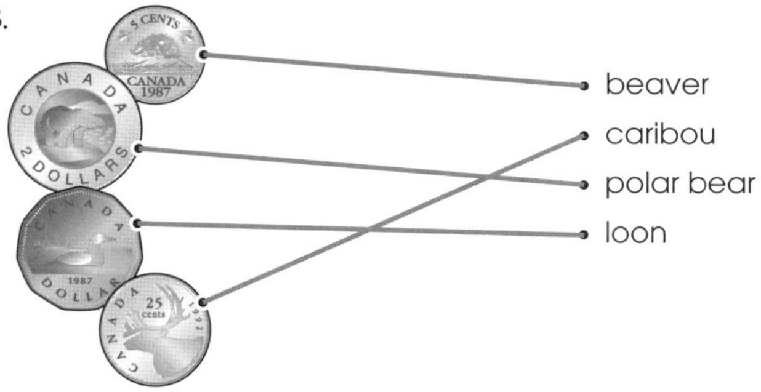

Test 13

A. 1. ocean ; A 2. parking lot ; B
   3. classroom ; B 4. waterfall ; A

B. 1. Cedar Lane and Pine Road
   2. Main Street and Nathan Street

Bonus
   It will get smaller.

Test 14

A. 1. C 2. C
   3. B 4. A

B. 1. reuse 2. reduce
   3. recycle 4. recycle
   5. reduce 6. reuse

Test 15

A. 1. E 2. G
   3. D 4. A
   5. B 6. C
   7. F

B.

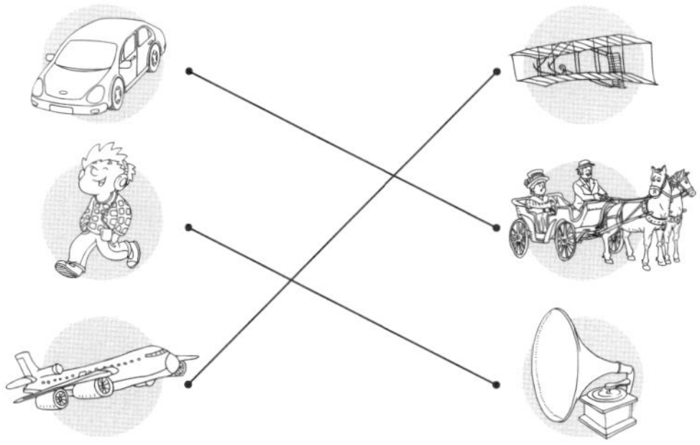

Bonus

Science

Test 1

A. eye ; see
nose ; breathe
tongue ; taste
hand ; touch
foot ; move

B. 1. flies ; wings
2. jumps ; legs

C. 1. teeth
2. hands / fingers
3. arms

Test 2

A. 1. smell
2. touch
3. taste
4. see
5. hear
6. smell
7. see
8. hear
9. taste
10. touch

B. 1. see ; hear
2. touch ; taste

C. 1. sunglasses
2. ear muffs
3. oven mitts

Test 3

A. B ; C ; E ; F

B. (Individual answers)

C. 1.

2.

D.

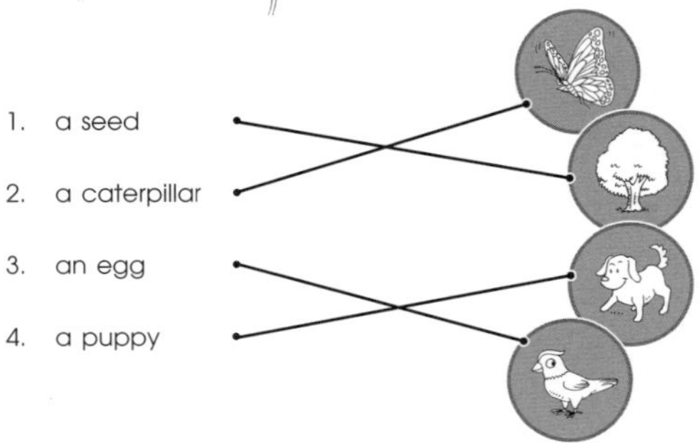

Test 4

A.

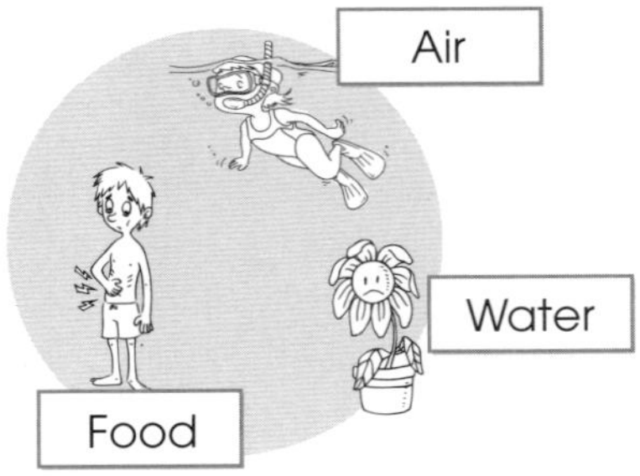

B. 1. water 2. food
3. air

C. 1-2. (Individual examples)

1.

2.

Bonus
rings

Test 5

A.

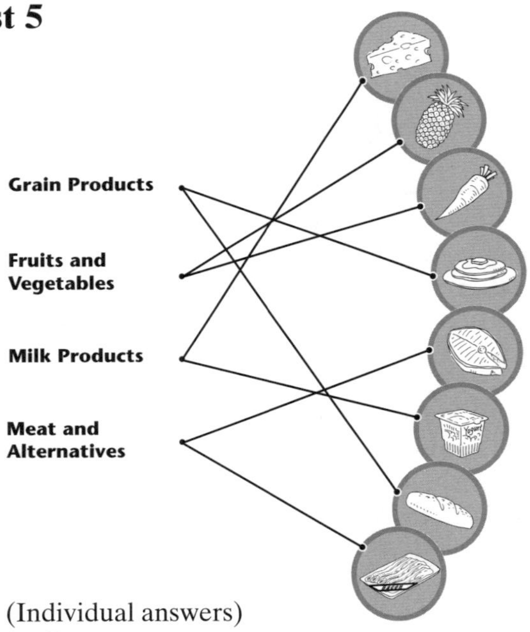

B. (Individual answers)

C. 1. Cross out: sausages
2. Cross out: butter
3. Cross out: lollipop
4. Cross out: pop

Test 6

A. 1.

2.

3.

4.

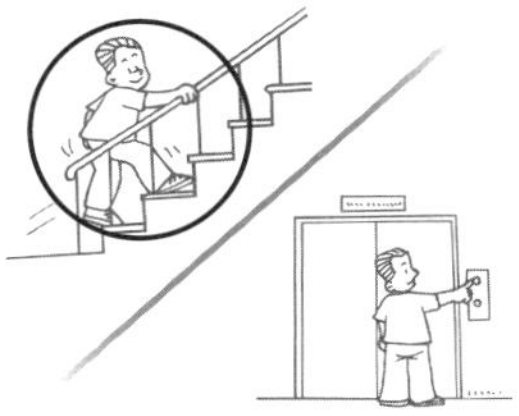

B. (Individual answer)
C. A ; B ; C
D. 1.

2.

3.

Test 7

A. (Individual examples)

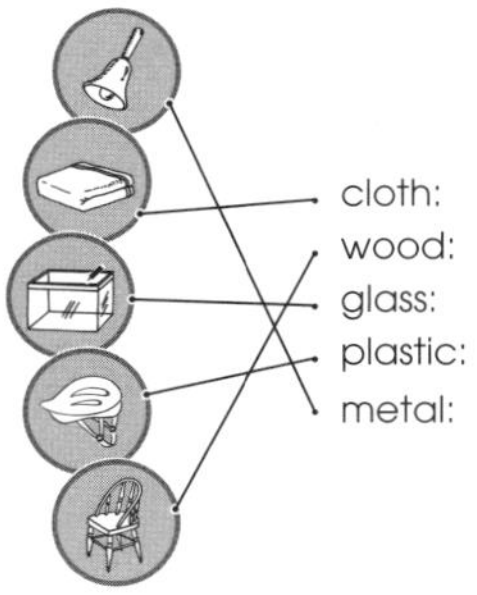

B. 1. B ; C 2. A ; C 3. A ; D
C. 1. glass ; metal
2. wood ; metal

Test 8

A. 1. feathers ; animals 2. metal ; the Earth
3. wood ; plants 4. plastic ; plants
B. 1. hard ; heavy
2. shiny ; sinks when placed in water

C. (Individual answers)
Bonus
No, because it would be too heavy.

Test 9

A.

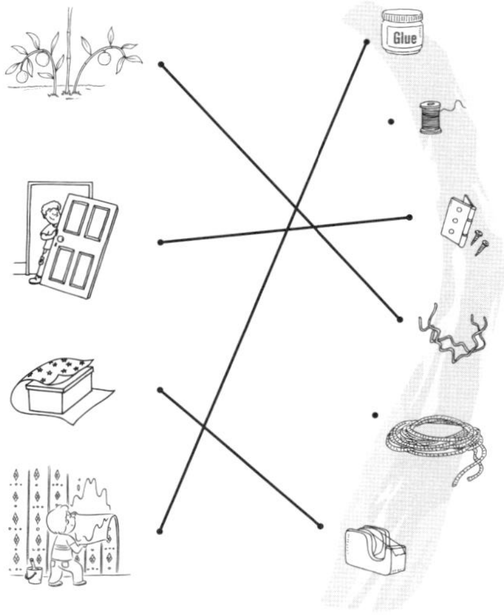

B. Draw zipper or buttons.
C. 1.

2.

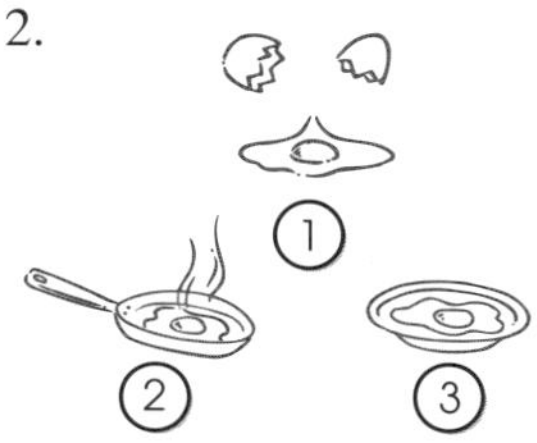

3. temperature

Test 10

A. 1. A 2. C 3. B
4. C 5. A
B.

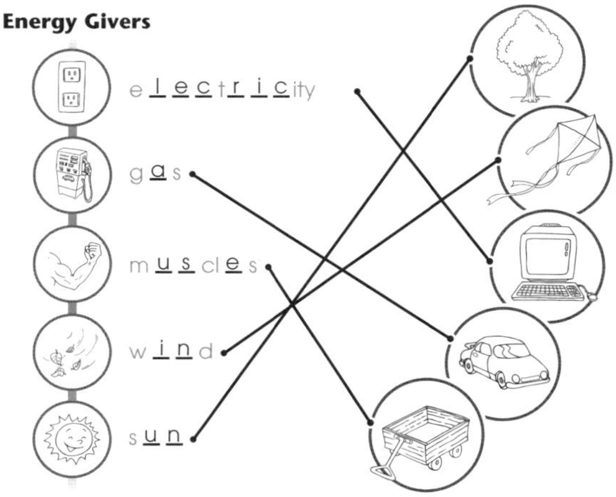

Bonus
electricity

Test 11

A. Check: A ; C ; E ; H
Cross out: B ; D ; F ; G
B. (Individual answers)
C. 1. A 2. B
D. 1. B 2. A

Test 12

A. Check: B ; D
Cross out: A ; C
B.
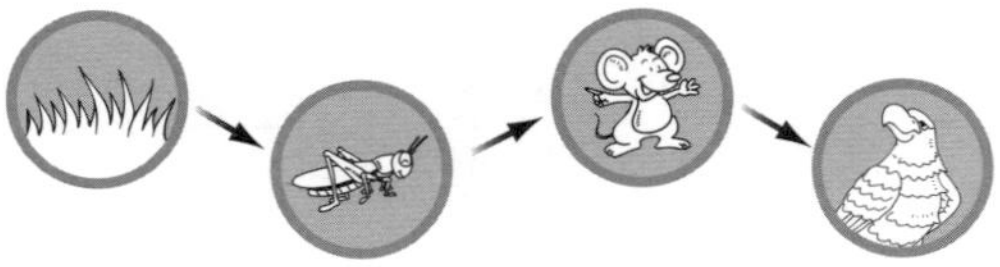

C. 1.

2.

D. D ; C ; A ; B

Test 13

A. 1.

2.

3.

4.

B. (Individual answers)
C.
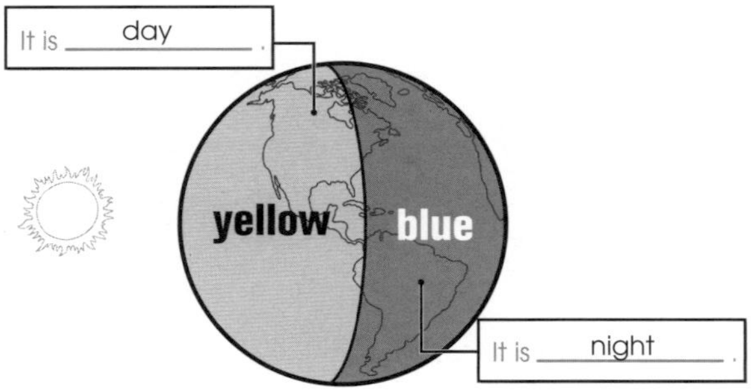

D. morning: B
evening : A

Test 14

A.
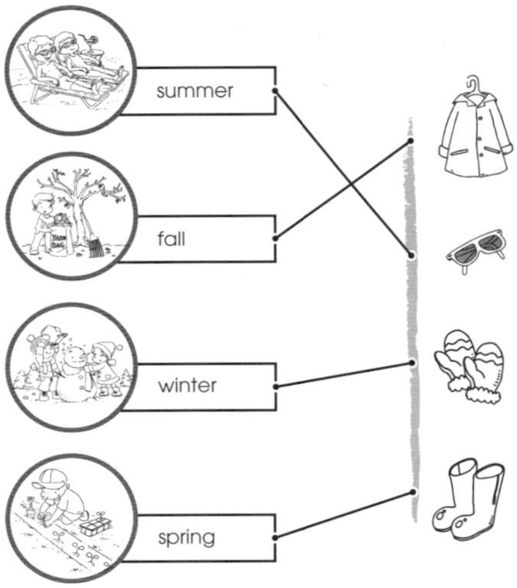

B. 1. winter
2. summer
3. spring
4. summer
5. fall
6. spring

Bonus
(Individual answer)

Test 15

A. (Individual answers)
B. A: winter
B: winter
C: summer
D: summer
C.
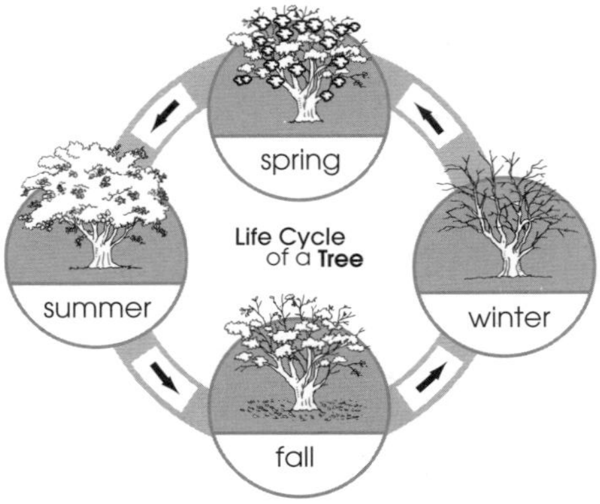

Bonus

(Individual answers)